AS/A LEVEL
STUDENT GUIDE

CW00920198

OCR

Media Studies

Component 2: Evolving Media

Jason Mazzocchi

HODDER
EDUCATION
AN HACHETTE UK COMPANY

The teaching content of this resource is endorsed by OCR for use with specification AS Level Media Studies (H009) and specification A Level Media Studies (H409). In order to gain OCR endorsement, this resource has been reviewed against OCR's endorsement criteria.

This resource was designed using the most up to date information from the specification. Specifications are updated over time which means there may be contradictions between the resource and the specification, therefore please use the information on the latest specification and Sample Assessment Materials at all times when ensuring students are fully prepared for their assessments.

Any references to assessment and/or assessment preparation are the publisher's interpretation of the specification requirements and are not endorsed by OCR. OCR recommends that teachers consider using a range of teaching and learning resources in preparing learners for assessment, based on their own professional judgement for their students' needs. OCR has not paid for the production of this resource, nor does OCR receive any royalties from its sale. For more information about the endorsement process, please visit the OCR website, www.ocr.org.uk.

Although every effort has been made to ensure that website addresses are correct at time of going to press, Hodder Education cannot be held responsible for the content of any website mentioned in this book. It is sometimes possible to find a relocated web page by typing in the address of the home page for a website in the URL window of your browser.

Hachette UK's policy is to use papers that are natural, renewable and recyclable products and made from wood grown in well-managed forests and other controlled sources. The logging and manufacturing processes are expected to conform to the environmental regulations of the country of origin.

Orders: please contact Bookpoint Ltd, 130 Park Drive, Milton Park, Abingdon, Oxon OX14 4SE. Telephone: (44) 01235 827720. Fax: (44) 01235 400401. Email education@bookpoint.co.uk Lines are open from 9 a.m. to 5 p.m., Monday to Saturday, with a 24-hour message answering service. You can also order through our website: www.hoddereducation.co.uk

ISBN: 978 1 5104 2950 5

© Jason Mazzocchi 2018

First published in 2018 by

Hodder Education, An Hachette UK Company, Carmelite House, 50 Victoria Embankment, London EC4Y 0DZ

Impression number   5   4   3   2   1

Year   2022 2021 2020 2019 2018

All rights reserved. Apart from any use permitted under UK copyright law, no part of this publication may be reproduced or transmitted in any form or by any means, electronic or mechanical, including photocopying and recording, or held within any information storage and retrieval system, without permission in writing from the publisher or under licence from the Copyright Licensing Agency Limited. Further details of such licences (for reprographic reproduction) may be obtained from the Copyright Licensing Agency Limited, www.cla.co.uk

Cover photo © Vasya Kobelev/Shutterstock

Typeset in India

Printed in Italy

A catalogue record for this title is available from the British Library.

MIX
Paper from
responsible sources
FSC™ C104740
FSC
www.fsc.org

Contents

Content Guidance

Section A: Media Industries and Audiences

Section B: Long-form Television Drama

■ Getting the most from this book

Study tips

Advice on key points in the text to help you learn and recall content, avoid pitfalls, and polish your exam technique in order to boost your grade.

Knowledge check

Rapid-fire questions throughout the Content Guidance section to check your understanding.

Knowledge check answers

1 Turn to the back of the book (page 99) for the Knowledge check answers.

Summaries

■ Each core topic is rounded off by a bullet-list summary for quick-check reference of what you need to know.

Practice questions

Commentary on the questions

Tips on what you need to do to gain full marks, indicated by the icon **e**

Sample student answers

Practise each question, then look at the student answers that follow.

Section A: Media Industries and Audiences

Practice question and sample answer: Film

Explain how films can be marketed to become global brands. Refer to the *Jungle Book* films in your answer. [15 marks]

e *The Jungle Book* (1967) and *The Jungle Book* (2016) are introductory case studies in understanding media institutions and audiences. In your response, use them as examples of institutional organisation and audience consumption, evaluating them as institutional texts. Aim to spend 25 minutes on this question.

Sample answer

The Jungle Book (1967) is an all-time Disney classic that has appealed to generations of audiences. At over 50 years of age this film is still well received by family audiences and has a universal appeal. This is no coincidence, but an example of the business strategy of Disney, a media company that successfully brands and distributes its products globally and across different film markets. The success of the film of course derives from the high quality of the product and the clever conversion of a popular literary text into a quality animated film, with its related tie-ins to theme parks, TV series and merchandise.

The Jungle Book (2016) also reflects a business strategy that has been successful for Disney as a media institution. Adaptation to a changing media environment – the online age – has meant that while traditional film practices remain in place, for example with the use of film posters and trailers, the company and its size, power and reach have been transformed to an even larger scale, with innovation in digital technologies and the ability to target traditional and non-traditional Disney audiences. *The Jungle Book* (2016) is an example of how the process of conglomerisation operates on a global scale. Not only has Disney produced a box office hit by remaking a classic from its vault, but it's also struck global licensing and merchandising deals that will provide multiple conduits of income for years to come. An example of how Disney marketed *The Jungle Book* so successfully was by using social media accounts, such as Facebook, Twitter and Instagram. In a move away from traditional marketing campaigns, Disney also uploaded an interactive movie poster on Snapchat and users could apply a framed 'Jungle Book' lens, which turned their faces into the snake Kaa. It could be argued that this successful formula has kept Disney Studios at the forefront of Hollywood film production. At the heart of any academic study of *The Jungle Book* (2016) compared to the 1967 version are these questions on how film is produced, distributed and consumed by media institutions and audiences – illustrated by the power, size and scale of a conglomerated media business.

e This is a detailed and thorough response that includes plenty of relevant content and considers well the comparison between two texts. It is clear and coherent in its arguments, logical and well organised – it would be a high-level answer.

Commentary on sample student answers

Find out how many marks each answer would be awarded in the exam and then read the comments (preceded by the icon **e**) following each student answer. Annotations that link back to points made in the student answers show exactly how and where marks are gained or lost.

■ About this book

This guide is for students following the OCR A Level Media Studies course. It deals with Component 2 Evolving Media and includes the study of media institutions and audiences and media contexts – historical, economic, political and social.

The main **Content Guidance** part of the guide provides details of the topics in Component 2 Section A Media Institutions and Audiences, including coverage of *The Jungle Book* (1967) and *The Jungle Book* (2016), *The Radio 1 Breakfast Show* and *Minecraft*. The Content Guidance goes on to offer information on Component 2 Section B on Long-form Television Drama.

Included within this part are links with media theory and contexts of production and consumption. Topic areas on Evolving Media examine key ideas and arguments, stating the main points of evaluation, and include the key concepts and key thinkers. Further information about academic theories and key thinkers can be found in the OCR 'Academic ideas and arguments (theories) for A Level' factsheet, accessible here: www.ocr.org.uk/images/421658-academic-ideas-and-arguments-factsheet.pdf. Key terms for the OCR specification are defined in the margin boxes in this section.

Practice questions and sample answers are given at the end of the study of each set media product for Section A and at the end of Section B, to show you the kind of questions you can expect in the Evolving Media exam. For each question a sample student-style response is given, along with a comment indicating levels of achievement (low, mid or high) and ideas for how to improve the response.

How to use this guide

As you study each set product for Component 2 Evolving Media in class, read the corresponding section from the Content Guidance to become more familiar with the topic. You should use these sections to complete your own revision notes on each product in Section A and Section B.

Once you have done this, attempt to address the sample question for each set product. When you have completed your answer, read the sample response and compare it with your own. This response and the comment that follows it can be used to amend and expand your revision notes.

The A Level specification is shown in detail on the OCR website: www.ocr.org.uk/qualifications/as-a-level-gce/as-a-level-gce-media-studies-h009-h409-from-2017 – follow the links to Media Studies A Level (H409).

Content Guidance

■ Section A: Media Industries and Audiences

This part of the course looks at media institutions and audiences. It is the most factual part of the A Level. Here is a summary of the OCR specification coverage for Evolving Media, Section A Media Institutions and Audiences:

Table 1.1 Summary of the OCR specification coverage for Section A Media Institutions and Audiences

Media form	Film	Radio	Video games
Set media products	The Jungle Book (1967) and The Jungle Book (2016)	The BBC Radio 1 Breakfast Show	Minecraft
Media industries	✓	✓	✓
Media audiences		✓	✓
Media contexts	Economic and historical	Economic, political and cultural	Economic and social

Questions 1 and 2 in the exam each carry 15 marks. These questions will be set on two of the three set products and you are advised to spend 25 minutes on each question. (To see an example of the question paper and mark scheme for Section A, please visit the OCR website.)

The nature of media institutions and audiences requires you to understand the relationship between the production of a media text and how it is consumed by an audience. You will explore a number of factors, including the historical and social cultural contexts of media products. Further, you will be introduced to key media terminology in relation to media production, ownership, distribution and marketing, digital technology and media audiences.

This section of the guide considers how past and present media practices are being transformed in an online age – how they are evolving and growing from traditional media practices. It begins with a case study on film, and then looks at radio and video games. Section B then looks at US and European long-form TV drama.

Film

The Jungle Book

As a part of the study of media industries you will make a comparative study of two set film texts:

- *The Jungle Book* (1967)
- *The Jungle Book* (2016)

The films need be studied in relation to both media contexts and media industries, and these can be exemplified by discussion of the production, distribution and exchange of the films. Your study of these films also needs to cover the economic and historical contexts of the film industry.

You need to study these set films in relation to the following subject content bullet points from the Media Industries section of the specification:

- The specialised and institutionalised nature of media production, distribution and circulation.
- The relationship of recent technological change and media production, distribution and circulation.
- The significance of patterns of ownership and control, including conglomerate ownership, vertical integration and diversification.
- How media organisations maintain, including through marketing, varieties of audiences nationally and globally.
- The impact of 'new' digital technologies on media regulation, including the role of individual producers.
- How processes of production, distribution and circulation shape media products.
- The impact of digitally convergent media platforms on media production, distribution and circulation, including individual producers.
- The role of regulation in global production, distribution and circulation.

The Jungle Book (1967 and 2016)

As a student of this topic you are being asked to identify and explain how media institutions' processes of production, distribution and circulation affect media forms and platforms. By understanding the subject content in the above bullet points, you will be able to evaluate how *The Jungle Book* (1967) is comparable to *The Jungle Book* (2016). According to the OCR specification:

> *The Jungle Book* (2016) has taken over 1 billion US dollars already at the cinema box office alone (and will generate more income as a DVD/Blu-ray disc and online). The film has a clear pattern of production, distribution and circulation that can be easily distinguished and is a film production from a major studio.
>
> *The Jungle Book* (1967) is a historically significant media product and film text. The 1967 film is currently one of the most successful films of all time (it has taken over 100 billion US dollars) and followed a traditional pattern of production, distribution and circulation, although it enjoyed a 'second life' on video and DVD.

(Source: OCR A Level Media Studies specification)

Study tip

Often an exam question will be written around a point from the specification. In this instance a question on *The Jungle Book* is going to be comparative and may be linked to production, distribution, exhibition and/or consumption.

Using both films for the focus of an industry study will allow you to consider how the film industry has changed from 1967 to the present day, in relation to:

- how each of the films was produced, distributed and circulated, including considerations of technological change
- the significance of patterns of ownership and economic factors.

The Jungle Book (1967)

The Jungle Book (1967) is over 50 years old. It is a very successful film and to date has grossed over $100 billion. *The Jungle Book* was made by Disney Studios under the production company of Walt Disney Productions, a famous film studio in Hollywood that specialises in animated cartoons. The film is often described as an animated musical comedy. Other Disney texts from the same director, Wolfgang Reitherman, include *One Hundred and One Dalmatians* (1961) and *The Sword in the Stone* (1963).

Figure 1.1 Film poster of *The Jungle Book* (1967)

According to the OCR Factsheet on *The Jungle Book*:

> Disney's animation studio had been responsible for developing many of the techniques and ways of working that became standard practices of traditional cel animation, pioneering the art of storyboarding and developing the use of the multiplane to create an early 3D-like effect.
>
> (Source: OCR Media Studies Factsheet: *The Jungle Book* 2018)

Study tip

According to the guidelines in the specification, textual analysis is **not** a requirement of the study or assessment of film as a media form, and theories of media industries do **not** need to be applied.

Study tip

Disney is an excellent case study of a global commercial media company. It contrasts both with *Minecraft*'s company Mojang, which is a relatively new media gaming company, and *The Radio 1 Breakfast Show* as an example of a product from a public not-for-profit broadcaster.

Knowledge check 1

How much has *The Jungle Book* (2016) grossed compared to the 1967 original film?

Cel A thin clear sheet of plastic that a drawing is transferred to.

The production of *The Jungle Book* (1967) involved a specialised and institutionalised method of media production, which for Disney is animation and is still crucial to the studio's brand identity to this day. *The Jungle Book* (1967) was produced by Walt Disney Studios and cost $4 million to make. Walt Disney Studios is an American film studio based in Hollywood; between 1937 and 2016 it produced 56 animation films. During this long history, Walt Disney Studios has been considered the best animation company in film production, and as recently as 2007 Walt Disney Animation Studios purchased Pixar Animation Studios. This is a typical characteristic of a **media conglomerate** that has enough money and power to take over its competitors. Disney is a global film entertainment company – a media institution, with a long history of acquiring media companies, especially for their animation and CGI techniques and use of digital technologies.

> **Media conglomerate** A media group or media institution that owns numerous companies involved in mass-media enterprises, such as television, radio, publishing, motion pictures, theme parks or the internet. Conglomerates are usually global in their size and reach.

Disney Studios is seen as a leader in animation and art direction, having developed many of the techniques, concepts and principles that had become the standard practices of animation by the 1960s. Its specialised animation processes involve highly creative filmmakers using labour-intensive techniques from development of a concept to product, for example story writing, animation, special effects animation, storyboarding, and so on. *The Jungle Book* (1967) is a prime example of such high-cost and top-quality animation.

Historical context

The 1967 film is important to Disney Studios' history – it is a magical landmark film that is among the best ever written for Disney and includes the Oscar-nominated songs 'The Bare Necessities' and 'I Wanna Be Like You'. The original soundtrack for *The Jungle Book* was also the first to achieve gold disc status in the USA for an animated feature film. *The Jungle Book* (1967) itself is premised on an imaginative interpretation of Rudyard Kipling's *The Jungle Book*, and the film credits a notable cast and production team that had been in place and had worked together in the studio – at this time still a family-run business – for a number of years.

Economic contexts

By the time *The Jungle Book* was released Disney was already a successful film company, and the Disney Corporation was diversifying into theme parks (Disneyland), television series and merchandising deals. These were set up through its distribution arm, Buena Vista, in 1953. In part this was Disney's reaction to the baby boom of the 1950s, and the expansion of its business interests in home entertainment focused on its television series.

The Jungle Book was released in October 1967 and grossed nearly $24 million on its first worldwide release, demonstrating how spectacularly Disney could generate revenue from overseas markets, namely by selling a truly American brand:

- The film was produced on a budget of $4 million and was the fourth highest grossing movie in 1967.
- *The Jungle Book* was re-released in cinemas in the USA in 1978, 1984 and 1990.
- It enjoyed European screenings throughout the 1980s, with a particularly strong German market.
- The film has been released on a number of occasions to home entertainment markets.

The success of the film exemplifies how Hollywood conquers not only the home market, but also the global market. This is typical of the Disney brand and the quality of films that the company makes. The film also offers an example of media translation as it has benefited from evolving digital technologies and developments in home entertainment. The following timeline of its re-releases illustrates how historically Disney has embraced technological change to 'exploit' its product:

- *The Jungle Book* was released in the United States in 1967.
- In 1991, it was released as part of the Walt Disney Classics collection – illustrating how a media institution benefits from a back catalogue of movies that can be resold to younger generations. Three years later the home video sales totalled 14.8 million copies. The aim was to price the Disney Classics movies so that every family could afford to buy a copy.
- A limited issue DVD was released in 1999 by Buena Vista Home Entertainment and there was a subsequent release as a two-disc DVD in 2007, marketed as a platinum edition to celebrate the film's 40th anniversary.
- In 2010 the film was released as a Blu-ray/DVD/digital copy combo-pack.

By periodically reviving its assets in this way, Disney gains longevity of sales. Each time it translates an animation classic via the latest media technology to make it available in a new format, the company captures the next generation who then commit to the brand loyalty. *The Jungle Book* (1967) is a good example of Disney's key business strategy of regularly re-releasing animated classics.

Most recently, *The Jungle Book* (1967) has been released as a digital download via iTunes and is available on streaming services such as Amazon Video and Google Play – demonstrating the 'legs' of a movie made over 50 years ago and the success of Disney as a media institution in reselling the brand over and over again to different generations.

The total gross for the movie is $141 million in the USA and $205 million worldwide.

Ownership, distribution and control

Making money out of producing films to be shown at the cinema is very difficult. This is because there are so many other media platforms the film can be sold by, for example, through merchandising. Media companies practise **vertical integration** in order to control and maximise efficiency of the supply and distribution of the product – not just as films, but also as television, soundtracks and merchandise and, in Disney's case, theme parks as well. This illustrates how **media synergy** can support the continuing presence of a film and so promote **horizontal integration** across media and business interests, for example Disney film characters being evident in its theme parks and Disney Stores.

The Jungle Book is an example of how important synergy and merchandising is to a media conglomerate as it commodifies a successful media text. Film producers take a percentage of merchandising revenue, often through **licensing deals**. It has been estimated that:

> **movie property owners like Disney probably receive at least ten per cent of the wholesale price as their share of the profits.**

(Source: Nick Lacey: *Media, Institutions and Audiences*, 2002)

Knowledge check 2

What is the name of the company that owns *The Jungle Book* (1967), and how much did the film cost to make?

Vertical integration When a media company owns different businesses in the same chain of production and distribution.

Media synergy Using a single-sourced idea to create multiple selling points and products.

Horizontal integration When a media company creates a chain of goods or services across different divisions, often subsidiaries of the same company.

Licensing deal A legal contract between two parties, which grants a deal over a brand or product.

The Disney model is an example of how a media conglomerate operates:

> Disney was an early master of synergy, persuading companies to tie in with its films' release, running a character merchandising department ... The producer of animated films used the popularity of his famous cartoon characters for a weekly show on ABC that served as an advertisement for his theme park. In turn, visiting Disneyland helped secure customers' brand loyalty to the Disney trademark for the future. This strategy of cross-promotion ... has become a basis for the Walt Disney Company's rapid growth.
>
> (Source: OCR Teacher Guide: *The Jungle Book* 1967 and 2016: Industries and audience)

Disney products offer a plethora of opportunities both for cross-promotional campaigns in co-operation with other companies and for in-house cross-promotion marketing strategies. Exploiting the popularity of its brand is today (as in the past) a major profit source for Disney.

The Jungle Book (2016)

The Jungle Book was produced by Walt Disney Pictures and directed by Jon Favreau, who had previously produced *Iron Man* and *Iron Man 2* under his production company, Fairview Entertainment. *The Jungle Book* (2016) is a fantasy adventure movie with a darker and more sinister interpretation of Kipling's stories, and is a shift away from the light-hearted, toe-tapping and joyful original 1967 animation.

Figure 1.2 Film poster of *The Jungle Book* (2016)

Knowledge check 3

Define what you understand by the terms 'vertical integration' and 'horizontal integration'.

Production

Given the estimated production budget of $175 million, above-the-line costs were high in relation to creative talent such as actors, directors, writers and producers. The casting and use of more than 30 stars for the voiceovers, including film actors such as Scarlett Johansson and Ben Kingsley, was just as important as in the 1967 film. Below-the-line costs relate to the pure production costs, including all the other crew who work on the film and all of the technical costs such as hiring equipment, building sets, insurance, transport, accommodation and special effects. On top of these comes the marketing budget, which significantly adds to a film's overall costs.

Like *The Jungle Book* (1967) the contemporary version is well thought out and was an expensive movie to produce. Using its successful business model Disney was able to rely on a tried and tested formula with *The Jungle Book*, targeting a global market and family audiences with a successful brand. As it had in its vaults already a successful 50-year-old film, Disney could remake one of its existing assets. In a decade when Disney had already had two expensive blockbuster flops (*John Carter* (2012) and *The Lone Ranger* (2013)), it made sense to remake a movie with a proven business track record and a secure audience. Granting Favreau room to experiment in the remake of *The Jungle Book* was only partly the answer – Disney wanted to create a visual spectacle that could easily translate across multiple territories or overseas/global markets.

The Jungle Book (2016) can be described as a live action/CGI film as it combines live action and animated animals interacting on screen. The animals and landscapes were created on computer by the British digital effects house MPC. *The Jungle Book* (2016) was:

> **Planned by Walt Disney Studios Chairman Alan Horn as one of a series of remakes of their classic properties: 'Hollywood makes lots of films for kids, but the Disney reboots may be one of the few safe bets. They revive classic characters for a new generation of kids, and their already smitten parents may be especially willing to shell out for related merchandise.'**
>
> (Source: OCR Media Studies Factsheet: *The Jungle Book* 2018)

The time was right in development of this film property to combine the animation trademark qualities of Disney with the latest digital technology (photorealistic rendering, computer-generated technology and motion capture). The **proliferation** of digital technology in film has been driving film production in recent years. With CGI the digital creation of characters, sets and locations helps create a reality within the film, enabling storytelling and CGI to provide even more fantastical features, for example the tiger in the boat scenes in *Life of Pi* (2012), where a computer-animated tiger gives the impression that it shares life in a boat with a young boy.

Within Hollywood there is the emphasis on spectacle, which tends to privilege some genres over others, for example action, sci-fi and fantasy. These types of films dominate studio budgets, marketing and distribution spends, and Disney is no different – especially when it has a history of being an early adopter of new media technologies.

Study tip

Being able to understand the historical and social context of both films and being able to contrast these will demonstrate a comprehensive understanding of the assessment objectives for this unit.

Reboot Reimagining a previously made film as a fresh film, which re-invigorates the past film in order to attract new fans and stimulate revenue. Can be a comparatively safe project for a studio aiming for new audiences.

Proliferation A rapid and widespread increase in use, in this case of technology.

Study tip

When writing about a media extract or product in an essay you need to demonstrate application of ideas. Locate any examples mentioned in this resource via the internet, as this will aid your understanding and develop your independent study skills.

Under the influence of its director, *The Jungle Book* (2016) was to persuade audiences to watch film in cinemas for an '**immersive experience**', and this demonstrates that Disney was willing to be creative and a market leader with its use of digital technologies across all levels – production, distribution and exhibition. This is not new in Disney's history, as its business model sees the potential for media synergy and cross-media products. This is one way the studio reduces risks and offers the potential to maximise profits through creation of additional non-film revenue streams, such as merchandising.

By working alongside other media companies, the synergistic benefits of cross-promotion are effectively doubled. Disney is able to strike deals to make film and TV spinoffs, from which it gains a substantial share of profits. Disney chose to use its subsidiary companies to distribute the film, effectively meaning this was done at no cost as the money was flowing around inside the conglomerate rather than being paid out to another party. Disney granted licences to other companies to produce merchandise related to *The Jungle Book* (2016), including some companies that are also Disney **subsidiaries**, and in so doing created additional non-film revenues and tie-ins. As both a vertically integrated company (distributing as well as producing films) and a horizontally integrated company (promoting its products across different media and non-media interests including the theme parks), Disney is in a powerful position to engage with a global audience using the internet as a distribution platform for its goods.

Distribution

Film distribution is the process of making a film available to the audience to view. This is normally the task of a professional **film distributor**. The sole distributor for *The Jungle Book* was Walt Disney Studio Motion Pictures, which is owned by the Walt Disney Company. It handles the theatrical release, marketing and promotion of films produced globally and has 18 bases in different regions of the world (Internet Movie Database).

After three years in the making from concept to product, *The Jungle Book* (2016) was released from April to July 2016 across 70 different national territories. The highly competitive business of launching and sustaining a film to the largest appropriate audience was timed by Disney for a summer film release, traditionally seen as coinciding with events for school-age children and family time.

The Jungle Book was released in North America in Disney Digital 3-D. This is Disney's brand name for three-dimensional films made and released by Disney exclusively using digital projection. The film was also released in RealD 3D, IMAX and IMAX 3D, with a worldwide opening figure for IMAX of $20.4 million from 901 IMAX screens, remarkable for a PG-rated film. In the USA 10 per cent of the screenings were in an IMAX format and the film grossed a total of $39 million in IMAX screenings worldwide. The film became a critical and commercial success, grossing over $966 million, making it the fifth highest grossing film of 2016 and the highest grossing film in Europe and the UK in that year. The production of the film in pristine or high-quality aspect ratios provided not only a premium product for the cinema, but also the opportunity to sell the film in its various formats further on down the distribution **value chain**.

Immersive experience
Relating to time and energy or occupying one's attention.

Subsidiaries
Companies that are owned or controlled by another company, which is called the parent company.

Film distributor
A company that determines the marketing strategy for a film and the media by which a film is to be exhibited or made available for viewing; it may also set the release date and define the release windows – in cinemas, according to region, and then on digital services, DVD and Blu-ray, and ultimately on streaming services and free-to-air broadcasts.

Value chain How value is added to a media product in its distribution, for example in exhibition and by merchandising.

The current trend for making theatrical release windows shorter between different countries is fuelled by the growing importance of non-theatrical revenue sources. At present DVD/Blu-ray sales account for almost twice the profit earned by theatrical exhibition. Historically, cinema has been the source of the highest revenue in the shortest time, cascading down through home exhibition, television and so on, in descending order of profitability. This is now changing, so that cinema is more like a shop window for non-theatrical sales and revenue.

Films usually open in cinemas first. This gives a product commercial value and creates further demand for viewing – especially in high-end technology formats. Following a big-screen run of approximately 16 weeks, films are released on a flexible timescale through other formats:

- home entertainment release, such as DVD, 3D Blu-ray, Blu-ray and digital HD
- PPV or subscription television, streaming and broadcast free-to-air TV
- as downloadable movies on Disney Anywhere, iTunes, Google Play and Amazon Video.

Film marketing

The Jungle Book had a very profitable value chain and was distributed as an output deal. Film distributors are involved with a film before production, advising on its marketability. A distribution agreement will also cover:

- the promotion in all media before and after release
- different cuts of a film necessary for different territories or cultures
- how the income for the release will be apportioned
- how far the distribution licence extends into ancillary markets such as home entertainment and TV.

The objective for film marketing is to create 'visibility' for an individual film and to engage interest in the audience. This is not an easy process when so many films, let alone other forms of competing entertainment, are vying for attention. As a result, interest in a film needs to be built to peak as the film opens at cinemas. Director Jon Favreau was aware of the technological interrelationship between the making of *The Jungle Book* and its promotion:

> What's interesting about the film is we are telling an old story with new technology, and that's bled over into other aspects of film and promotion ... We had an extremely sophisticated technological landscape that we were dealing with day to day as we created the film. Now, as we explore the means by which we share it with people, technology seemed like a very inherent part of the whole live action *Jungle Book* movie.

(Source: OCR Media Studies Factsheet: *The Jungle Book* 2018)

Early release windows create problems with **substitutability** (that is, they cannibalise later sales), but they can benefit from complementarity (there is a spillover of marketing and word-of-mouth buzz). In any case, theatrical releases are now frequently loss leaders for a stream of subsequent related formats and products, but this was not the case with *The Jungle Book* (2016).

Knowledge check 4

Identify the subsidiary that distributes Disney's products.

Knowledge check 5

Identify two main purposes of a film distributor.

Substitutability When a film shown in cinemas is then made available on DVD, as pay-per-view and on streaming/subscription services for audiences to consume.

Figure 1.3 Jon Favreau, director of *The Jungle Book* (2016)

Study tip

Using quotes from a student book is not a requirement for the assessed unit, but engagement with the ideas that such books offer will help you understand the set films.

Different elements of film marketing that attract audience attention for the film include:

- word of mouth – social recommendation is the most effective trigger for cinema attendance and can give a film 'legs', so interest remains high for weeks after release
- posters – choosing and using an image to distil the essence of a film
- trailers – the most cost-effective form of promotion, normally shown prior to another film with a similar target audience
- social media messages – for example *The Jungle Book* 2016 Facebook, Twitter and Instagram accounts.

Online and digital marketing in the form of an official website, social networking sites and online video sharing can all be used to promote and publicise a film. User-generated material, forums and insider film sites can create problems with controlling how a film is reported to an audience. The official Disney accounts, however, released teasers and 'the making of' photos and videos in the months before the theatrical release. The marketing campaign kept up the promotion for the DVD and downloads releases.

> Disney made several smart marketing choices during the lead-in to the release of The Jungle Book that helped build hype and buzz for the movie. They combined typical marketing approaches, special opportunities available only to Disney and a few unique techniques and messaging particular to this film ... The result was maximum marketing impact.
>
> (Source: www.waxmarketing.com, May 12 2016)

This extract highlights the importance of sharing the film concept early, which is obviously an invaluable promotional tool, and a range of media technologies were successfully used to spread this concept to global audiences. As Disney could no longer rely solely on traditional media to convince its older audiences to watch a film about cartoon characters, it used CGI on social media to sell and promote the movie. Disney also used bloggers and entertainment news sites to hammer home a key point: Favreau had employed sophisticated film-making techniques to create animal characters.

Below are some of the promotional events that were used to help market *The Jungle Book* (2016):

1   Disney made concerted efforts to promote the film to male audiences. Trailers aired on TV sports networks like ESPN and highlighted that the film came from the same studio that made the *Pirates of the Caribbean* series, rather than *Cinderella*. An extended 3D trailer was also played at screenings of *Star War: The Force Awakens*.

2   Studio marketers targeted Hispanic audiences by teaming up with the American Spanish-language TV network Univision. *Jungle Book* characters and clips were included in various programmes on the TV network for five weeks leading up to the film's release.

3   Social media were used effectively, focusing on showcasing the immersive world of *The Jungle Book*. For example, a promotional video on Facebook allowed users a 360° view at part of the film's jungle.

4   Disney took advantage of its huge global presence to promote *The Jungle Book*. The studio's multiple theme parks showed sneak-peak footage of the film with the director, John Favreau, giving introductions to audiences.

5   *Jungle Book* themed merchandise was stocked in Disney stores in theme parks and malls and specially designed *Jungle Book* sand sculptures were built in Disney's Animal Kingdom park in Florida.

(Source: adapted from www.waxmarketing.com, May 12 2016)

Technology, social media and exchange

Disney's marketing campaign was intertwined with the use of social media and created an immersive world of *The Jungle Book*, for example via:

- Disney's interactive website for *The Jungle Book*
- special promotions at IMAX cinemas
- a touring virtual-reality experience and 360° Facebook video emphasising the *Avatar*-like world of its jungle
- an initial trailer, teased with a seven-second clip on Instagram
- a full-length trailer on YouTube
- a special extended 3D trailer in select IMAX cinemas, shown in front of *Star Wars: The Force Awakens* screenings
- an interactive movie poster produced for the Snapchat Discover platform.

Study tip

Take time to independently research promotional examples referred to in this resource. Exploring these online will act as an *aide memoire* for the points made here.

Knowledge check 6

Recall two examples of marketing and promotional devices that Disney used in the promotion of *The Jungle Book* (2016).

According to the director Jon Favreau in an interview, the teaser marketing campaign for *The Jungle Book* (2016) was crucial to the success of a film designed to bring a classic tale to a new, more tech-savvy generation.

Little by little, fans were shown new sections of the film to help them know what to expect, while also not giving much away. Using this strategy kept potential viewers interested enough to go to the cinema to watch the film, while ensuring it was still new and exciting when they did. The goal was to create a fully immersive world where the viewer would forget that the scenery and most of the cast were computer-generated, and instead be drawn in by the virtual world.

Technology became a prominent part of the marketing process, and online (social) media technologies ensured that audiences were able to co-opt into the campaign and live the marketing experience.

It is important to remember in discussion of the marketing of *The Jungle Book* (2016) that Disney's budget would have been huge and, as well as new marketing practices, was still reliant upon the old: the film poster, trailer, publicity still, promotions, previews, premiere events, download activities and education packs.

The power of Disney to promote *The Jungle Book* is most visible with the TV advertising and cross-promotion of the film. The movie ran its first global TV spot during the US Super Bowl. The film's Super Bowl spot achieved the second highest brand mentions of the movies advertised during the game. It also came in second among films on a ranking of Facebook advertising engagement. Technology and nostalgia continued to be the main components of the marketing campaign, alongside exploitation of Favreau's status as Hollywood star-turned-director and his wish to do something technically innovative with the film.

This quote from the OCR Factsheet aptly summarises the significance of the marketing of *The Jungle Book* (2016):

> **Stepping back to look at it, Disney has developed a marketing strategy not dissimilar to a political campaign ... Disney has pulled off some big, complex marketing in the past, but nothing quite as perfect and impressive as what it accomplished with *The Jungle Book*.**
>
> (Source: OCR Media Studies Factsheet: *The Jungle Book* 2018)

Study tip

Use as wide a range of examples as possible in any answer you give – US examples are equally as valid as examples from the UK.

Audience

The Jungle Book (2016) was an overwhelming success for Disney Studios. As a product of this global brand it succeeded in attracting a wide range of age groups, not just the under-16s or its traditional family audience, to see the film. Disney's achievement in re-making a Disney classic is phenomenal, in part due to the technology involved and the reinterpretation of the characters and the narrative, but also to the ability of the conglomerate to market and distribute the product and to value its audience. This is reflected in the global box office returns for the film, over $966 million, and in the critical acclaim it received – winning the Academy Award for Best Visual Effects. *The Jungle Book* product has also been successfully commodified through the Disney Store.

Depending on the genre and theme of a film, distributors will look to arrange promotion with third-party companies. The range of merchandise includes:

- product tie-ins, which generate displays for the film in shops or restaurants or on packaging
- merchandising such as toys, clothing, soundtracks and video games
- theme park visits
- premium cinema experiences, such as IMAX or Dolby Vision 3D
- a soundtrack album
- TV rights
- Blu-ray and DVD releases and video streaming.

The film enjoyed unrivalled success in its marketing and distribution to India, China and Europe and other overseas markets – a characteristic of Disney Studios.

In addition the film was made appealing to action-adventure fans and animation and special effects viewers. These are identifiable as middle-aged and male movie-goers – not typically associated with *The Jungle Book*'s audience. This is in part due to the use of visual effects and digital technology.

Moreover, Disney as an adopter of media technologies used social networking to promote the film, triggering audience engagement and interaction with its marketing strategies. This effective utilisation of the company's resources and power created an immersive viral campaign that was consumable by all age ranges when allied with traditional marketing strategies. Taking this with the merchandising for children, the targeting of nostalgia, the synergy of the movie and male audience demographics, it is clear that *The Jungle Book* certainly succeeded in maintaining its audience in a transforming and connected global media environment.

Any media institution's success is dependent on old and new audiences at the level of production. *The Jungle Book* (2016) is the successful reboot of an old classic story premised upon the creative success of its animation and the use of CGI, which dominates contemporary Hollywood film making. The audience needs levels of engagement not only in the text itself, but also in the distribution and **spreadability** of the brand – and Disney's role in this is to create a fan culture. Disney has also adapted to an online age. Developing the film concept alongside social media and interactive technologies, it has not only been creative with its production but also with how the film is marketed and exchanged by traditional family audiences and new audience segments.

Spreadability The wide distribution and circulation of information on a media platform.

Summary

- The comparison between the two different versions of *The Jungle Book* (1967 and 2016) reveals the characteristics of Disney as a global media brand.
- It is a conglomerate company that has the ability to produce, distribute and exhibit film texts on a global scale.
- The company specialises in a range of films, including animation, and is considered a leader in the use of digital and special effects.
- Disney's success has been its adaptability to emerging digital technologies, the export of its product to global markets and the selling of its brand through horizontal integration into publications, theme parks, TV channels, merchandise, and so on.

Practice question and sample answer: Film

Explain how films can be marketed to become global brands. Refer to the *Jungle Book* films in your answer.

[15 marks]

(e) *The Jungle Book* (1967) and *The Jungle Book* (2016) are introductory case studies in understanding media institutions and audiences. In your response, use them as examples of institutional organisation and audience consumption, evaluating them as institutional texts. Aim to spend 25 minutes on this question.

Sample answer

The Jungle Book (1967) is an all-time Disney classic that has appealed to generations of audiences. At over 50 years of age this film is still well received by family audiences and has a universal appeal. This is no coincidence, but an example of the business strategy of Disney, a media company that successfully brands and distributes its products globally and across different film markets. The success of the film of course derives from the high quality of the product and the clever conversion of a popular literary text into a quality animated film, with its related tie-ins to theme parks, TV series and merchandise.

The Jungle Book (2016) also reflects a business strategy that has been successful for Disney as a media institution. Adaptation to a changing media environment – the online age – has meant that while traditional film practices remain in place, for example with the use of film posters and trailers, the company and its size, power and reach have been transformed to an even larger scale, with innovation in digital technologies and the ability to target traditional and non-traditional Disney audiences. *The Jungle Book* (2016) is an example of how the process of conglomerisation operates on a global scale. Not only has Disney produced a box office hit by remaking a classsic from its vault, but it's also struck global licensing and merchandising deals that will provide multiple conduits of income for years to come. An example of how Disney marketed *The Jungle Book* so successfully was by using social media accounts, such as Facebook, Twitter and Instagram. In a move away from traditional marketing campaigns, Disney also uploaded an interactive movie poster on Snapchat and users could apply a framed 'Jungle Book' lens, which turned their faces into the snake Kaa. It could be argued that this successful formula has kept Disney Studios at the forefront of Hollywood film production. At the heart of any academic study of *The Jungle Book* (2016) compared to the 1967 version are these questions on how film is produced, distributed and consumed by media institutions and audiences – illustrated by the power, size and scale of a conglomerated media business.

(e) This is a detailed and thorough response that includes plenty of relevant content and considers well the comparison between two texts. It is clear and coherent in its arguments, logical and well organised – it would be a high-level answer.

Radio

The BBC Radio 1 Breakfast Show

The specification requires you to study one episode of *The BBC Radio 1 Breakfast Show*, from September 2017 onwards. You need to know how the show operates within the media industry and how its audiences are targeted. In the online age, radio has been transformed and the style and content of *The BBC Radio 1 Breakfast Show* exemplifies this. The key agent of change is media convergence, and you need to understand how the show has adapted to both technological and cultural change. According to Julian McDougall (2008), a media institution refers to companies and organisations that provide media content (in this instance a radio show), whether for profit, public service or other motive. As you will see from this section, Radio 1 is a not-for-profit public service broadcaster. This section requires you to understand the nature of production, distribution and consumption of *The BBC Radio 1 Breakfast Show*. In August 2018, Nick Grimshaw left the show and was succeeded by Greg James. The following material primarily relates to the show as it was when presented by Nick Grimshaw.

Significance

On 30 September 2017, *The BBC Radio 1 Breakfast Show* celebrated its 50th anniversary. When the show was launched in 1967 it offered a diet of pop music and was described by the *Radio Times* as 'the swinging new radio service'. It was set up as an alternative to the two existing BBC radio channels, BBC Radio 2 and Radio 4, at a time when there was no breakfast TV and no independent radio stations. *Radio 1 Breakfast* is still considered the flagship programme of the radio station, and even today a change of presenter on this programme – such as occurred in August 2018 – draws much media attention. In 1967, BBC Radio 1 was established at the request of the government following the banning of pirate radio stations. In line with all BBC channels, it cannot broadcast commercials and is financed through a licence fee under a **public service remit**.

Political context: the BBC as a media institution

The British Broadcasting Corporation (BBC) is a national **media institution** that was formed in 1927 under Lord Reith. It has a commitment to serve the public's interest. The BBC has ten radio stations covering the whole of the UK (including Radio 1, producer of *The Radio 1 Breakfast Show*), six stations in Wales, Scotland and Northern Ireland, and 40 local radio stations serving defined areas of England. Each station has a different remit, content, style and target audience. The target audience of Radio 1 is 15–29 years old and interested in a broad range of contemporary music and speech.

BBC Radio is funded by a **licence fee**. The licence that it operates is quite unique and is symbolic of a public service not-for-profit organisation. Radio 1's remit under this licence describes the most important characteristics of Radio 1, including how it contributes to the BBC's public purposes. Radio 1's remit is also to offer a range of new music, to support emerging artists (especially those from the UK) and to provide a platform for live music. Its news, documentaries and advice campaign offerings should cover areas of relevance to young adults.

Public service remit
The BBC is a public service organisation and serves the nation's interests. This public service remit is set out by Royal Charter and Agreement and at its core is the mission to inform, educate and entertain.

Media institution The underlying principles and values according to which many social and cultural practices are structured and co-ordinated by an organisation.

Licence fee A fee payable by the public for watching broadcast TV in the UK. It helps fund BBC TV and radio.

Knowledge check 7

Who is the target audience for BBC Radio 1?

Key provisions of BBC Radio 1

The service licence lies at the foundation of the broadcasting of *The Radio 1 Breakfast Show* and its key non-commercial characteristics. According to the BBC website, Radio 1 is available every day for general reception in the UK on FM, DAB digital radio and digital television platforms, and it also offers its broadcast content online. Many of the underlying principles of BBC Radio are found within the programming of *Radio 1 Breakfast*, which includes the following key points in its broadcast:

1   BBC content can be streamed via the internet, or multiple episodes of first-run series (known as 'series stacking') can be **downloaded** via BBC iPlayer Radio. For example, under the current presenter Greg James, 'The Greg James Podcast' with extracts from *Radio 1 Breakfast* is brought to the audience daily after the show and features the funniest clips and highlights from celebrity guests and music artists. This on-demand service is a free provision under the licence fee and is set up as a subscription service.

2   Programmes can be streamed on demand for a limited period after broadcast, for example, every Friday listeners to *The BBC Radio 1 Breakfast Show* were offered a free download of the Nixtape when Nick Grimshaw presented the show.

3   Video on BBC Online, and on other providers' platforms on demand, is made available, for example short streamed video interviews embedded into the website of *The BBC Radio 1 Breakfast Show.*

4   A limited number of special events may be streamed live, and a limited amount of content is made available online only, for example on the Galleries page on the iPlayer webpage. This includes events such as Wimbledon or Children in Need.

To support these features BBC Radio had a service budget of £34.7 million for 2016/17 and attracts 6 million listeners.

The aims of BBC Radio 1 broadcasting

Radio 1's daytime programmes, including *The Radio 1 Breakfast Show*, **broadcast** a mix of music, information and entertainment. Radio 1's programmes exhibit some or all of the following characteristics:

- high quality
- original
- challenging
- innovative
- engaging
- nurturing of UK talent.

The Mission of the BBC is to act in the public interest, serving all audiences through the provision of impartial, high-quality and distinctive output and services which inform, educate and entertain. As part of this, it pursues the delivery of a diverse range of music and output on its radio programmes to its multicultural audience, some of it innovative and occasionally challenging.

Download The act or process of downloading data in the form of text, audio or video.

Knowledge check 8

Identify three characteristics of *The BBC Radio 1 Breakfast Show* that demonstrate the BBC's provision of a public service.

Study tip

Demonstrate knowledge and understanding of the theoretical framework of media by explaining how political, cultural and economic contexts influence the status of popular music radio programming, in this case by understanding the public service offered by BBC Radio 1.

Broadcast To transmit a programme or some information by radio, television or internet. Broadcast programming (scheduling) is the practice of organising and/or ordering broadcast media programmes in a daily, weekly, monthly, quarterly or season-long schedule.

Here are the five public purposes of the BBC set out by the 2017 Royal Charter that are reflected in the production and broadcasting of *The Radio 1 Breakfast Show*:

1 **To show the most creative, highest quality and distinctive output and services.** Radio 1's daytime programmes offer a mix of music, information and entertainment and use an extensive playlist to introduce unfamiliar and innovative songs alongside more established tracks, for example the promotion of Live Lounge as a music feature.

2 **To provide impartial news and information to help people understand and engage with the world around them.** Speech programmes, including documentaries and social action campaigns, form an integral part of the schedule. This includes broadcast news during its daytime output that is accurate, impartial and independent. For example, *The Radio 1 Breakfast Show* provides (via Newsbeat) news that is aimed at its target audience.

3 **To support learning for people of all ages.** BBC Radio 1 contributes significantly to this purpose for its audience, primarily through its social action output, its regular advice programme, its documentaries and its vocational initiatives, for example the BBC Academy.

4 **To reflect, represent and serve the diverse communities of all of the United Kingdom's nations and regions and, in doing so, support the creative economy across the United Kingdom.** BBC Radio 1 fulfils this purpose for its audience through its extensive live events schedule. This connects the station directly with its listeners and reflects the diverse range of music enjoyed around the UK, for example the BBC Big Weekend event. **Interactive** forums allow listeners to share experiences and discuss areas of common interest, including music.

5 **To reflect the United Kingdom, its culture and values to the world.** Radio 1 plays its part in this purpose primarily by offering UK audiences access to the best global musical talent and coverage of significant international music events.

(Source: adapted from www.bbc.co.uk/aboutthebbc/insidethebbc/whoweare/publicpurposes, 2018)

Cultural contexts

BBC Radio champions UK music across all musical genres, and being playlisted remains a milestone for artists' careers in reaching out to millions of music fans.

Radio 1 is important for popular music, for artists and fans alike. As a flagship programme of the station, *The BBC Radio 1 Breakfast Show* is a prime example of this. Throughout its history, its format has been constructed around a strong presenter personality. Such personality-led shows have been an integral part of British media culture since the 1960s.

Study tip

Applying the public purposes of the BBC remit found in features of *The Radio 1 Breakfast Show* will demonstrate your understanding of how the principles of a media institution can be applied to its content.

Knowledge check 9

Why is broadcasting important for the BBC as a media institution?

Interactive A two-way flow of information between computer users.

Production

The Radio 1 Breakfast Show is broadcast live on air on weekdays from 6:30 a.m. to 10:00 a.m. It is available on FM, DAB, Freeview, Freesat, Virgin, Sky or online via BBC iPlayer Radio (including via phone or tablet app) where it can be heard live or streamed for 30 days. The show has its own website displaying a strong branding. The show is produced by the BBC at Broadcasting House in London and currently attracts 6 million listeners. The following BBC Academy podcast offers a useful insight into the production of the programme: www.bbc.co.uk/academy/articles/art20170619095219011 It addresses the following topics:

- the different responsibilities of presenters and producers
- the preparation that goes into making each programme
- what is most challenging and most enjoyable about working on the show
- team dynamics
- ways to get your first break in radio.

Study tip

Using links and commentaries online will enable you to gain a greater knowledge and understanding and aid you with the context of the production of popular music radio programming.

Knowledge check 10

How many listeners does *The Radio 1 Breakfast Show* have?

Figure 1.4 Broadcasting House in London

Content

Radio is essentially a non-visual medium that relies on the listener. Its messages necessarily rely on noise and silence, on the nature of its language and jokes, and on the ways in which its audience interact with it. *The Radio 1 Breakfast Show* depends on the presenter as the programme lead and this has historically been reflected in the production of the programme.

The characteristics of the show today in terms of the structure and flow of the radio broadcast – the presenter, **stings**, radio idents, interviews, phone-ins, competitions, music and, importantly, the regular news bulletins and sports updates – were also present in the daily flow of *Radio 1 Breakfast Shows* from the past. Under its public service remit, BBC Radio must broadcast at least one hour of daytime news each weekday, including two extended bulletins, and provide regular daytime bulletins at weekends. Newsbeat is produced by BBC News and is the dedicated news programme for BBC Radio 1 and BBC Radio 1Xtra. It differs from the BBC's other news programmes, however, in its remit to provide news tailored specifically for a younger audience.

Playlists

At the heart of *The Radio 1 Breakfast Show* is its popular music. This is produced through the tradition of creating **playlists**. The prestigious Radio 1 playlist has for decades dominated the shape of the British music charts and today remains at the heart of Radio 1's commitment to informing and entertaining the nation, especially as a scheduled audio alternative medium to news-dominated breakfast media culture. The Radio 1 playlist is decided in a meeting during the week leading up to the broadcast. The vast majority of music heard throughout the day on Radio 1 is from the playlist. It is made up of 42 songs that are played on rotation throughout the week. The number of plays a song gets is based on which part of the playlist it is on.

The playlist breaks down as follows:
- A List: These are the songs that are played the most, around 30 times in a week.
- B List: Music on this list gets around 15 plays per week.
- C List: Music on this list gets around 6 plays a week.
- BBC Introducing: This section of the playlist showcases brand new and under-the-radar artists, championed by BBC Introducing. They tend to get 6 plays in a week, but only remain on the playlist for one week.

By having four distinct playlists, BBC Radio 1 enables a diverse range of music – new, established and older – to gain airplay. It plays established artists alongside new ones – using both existing popular/mainstream music such as Taylor Swift and newer artists.

The Radio 1 Breakfast Show is required to demonstrate a 'distinctive' output of content compared to commercial radio. This affects the style and format of *The Radio 1 Breakfast Show* and its commitment to its target audience of under-30s. The importance of the playlist to the station is signalled by the fact that there is a webpage (www.bbc.co.uk/radio1/playlist) dedicated to Radio 1 playlists, which helps reference and trend popular music.

Running order

The OCR specification requires you to have studied a whole episode of *The BBC Radio 1 Breakfast Show* in detail. Listening to an episode will enable you to understand the production of the show and how it functions for its audience. You will not be required to analyse the show textually but you will be expected to make reference to

Sting A sound or short musical phrase used on radio to punctuate the programme, for example to introduce a regular feature.

Playlist A list of recordings to be played on the air by a radio station; also a similar list used for organising a personal digital music collection.

Knowledge check 11

How many playlists does Radio 1 have? And how many plays would a song on each receive?

examples from the key episode you have studied. Figure 1.5 shows an extract from an OCR Factsheet, where the author has deconstructed an episode format with brief notes on the running order. The episode format is from when it was presented by Nick Grimshaw.

6.30	News and weather
6.33	Programme ident; NG's intro; two tracks plus stings (a sting is a short jingle)
6.40	Sting. NG gives out contact details for audience to call in; track
6.43	Intro to the studio crew (producer and news presenter). Live studio chat between the three of them and discuss what's coming up. Announce celebrity guest coming at 8am
6.47	Track
6.50	Trail for a BBC Three drama
6.51	Track
6.54	Gives out text number; reads out listener messages while they are on the way to work; chat with studio crew
6.57	Track
	Station ident NG invites audience to choose a track after 8am
7.00	Radio 1 Newsbeat (news, sport, weather)
7.04	Timecheck, trail of Sunday's programme, rundown of next half an hour
7.06	Tracks, stings and idents
7.15	NG trails lunchtime programme; chats to listener on phone who chooses next track
7.20	Track
7.23	NG chat with listener; reading texts
7.24	Radio 1 Ident, tracks and sting; announce what's coming up
7.30	Radio 1 Newsbeat (news, sport, weather)
7.33	Radio 1 ident; track
7.36	Trail Entertainment news
7.37	Track
7.40	Radio 1 Ident, trail later guests;
	Entertainment news
7.45	Track; Trail guests; track
7.52	Radio 1 Ident; trail Live Lounge with a live phone interview with the artist
7.57	Track; trail Live Lounge and studio guest coming on at 8

Figure 1.5 OCR Media Studies Factsheet showing an episode format deconstructed

Source: OCR Media Studies Factsheet: *The BBC Radio 1 Breakfast Show* 2017)

The running order of *The BBC Radio 1 Breakfast Show* reflects the dominance of music track listings and the flow of the programme, with minor features on BBC programmes. Grimshaw, a media celebrity in his own right and the 'voice' of the show, provided familiarity and recognition for the audience. Importantly, the exemplar running order in Figure 1.5 includes a range of British music and content promoting British music, celebrity interviews, news items and quizzes/games that are required to demonstrate a 'distinctive' output of content compared to other stations.

Content features

The output of *The Radio 1 Breakfast Show* is shaped and styled by the presence of the presenter. So, in a selected episode presented by Nick Grimshaw, there is a strong focus on conversation and then on the credibility of the music, as reflected in this list of some of Grimshaw's show's content features:

- Call or Delete – a game Grimshaw carried on from his previous show on Radio 1, where celebrity guests choose either to prank-call a contact on their phone or to delete their number altogether
- The Nixtape – 30 minutes of party-orientated music selected by Grimshaw, before a DJ comes in to mix listener requests to close the week
- Happy Monday – half an hour of uplifting songs on Monday mornings
- Showquizzness – an irreverent daily quiz based around pop culture
- Happy Hardcore FM – listeners screaming over happy hardcore beats
- The Waking Up Song – celebrities encouraging listeners to get out of bed.

Popular and innovative music

The vital ingredient for *The Radio 1 Breakfast Show* is popular music. In the age of the internet radio has changed – national boundaries to music are abandoned and different audience segments seek music options in a global 'music jukebox'. Radio 1, however, continues to show its commitment to showcasing both established and emerging artists. According to Colin Lester, manager of the artist Craig David, Radio 1 is still the number one discovery place of music, for instance discovering the Arctic Monkeys.

Lester goes on to explain that although the internet has changed forever the way the music industry works, radio is still at the heart of it, and Radio 1's playlist stands above those of other stations. He suggests that the internet works hand in hand, or in symbiosis, with radio in order to connect radio, music, artists and audiences. Media institutions cannot ignore this but must adapt to and link with it.

Success for *The Radio 1 Breakfast Show* is dependent on reflecting what its target audience wants to listen to and on coping with changing audience use and exchange. Music choices for the *Breakfast Show* are taken from the Radio 1 playlist, which is compiled using a combination of editorial judgement by Radio 1 staff and data from a number of digital platforms. Radio 1 is a multi-genre radio station that showcases the best in new music, be it chart hits or artists championed by the DJs. Diversity and choice in the show are driven not by traditional chart music, but by a desire to be innovative and at the cutting edge with its music programming.

Study tip

From your study of one whole episode of *The Radio 1 Breakfast Show*, note as many content features from the programme as possible. Discussing these in relation to the Media Industries and Audiences question will generate marks.

Knowledge check 12

Identify two examples of features on *The Radio 1 Breakfast Show* that attract the audience.

Symbiosis A mutually beneficial relationship, or working hand in hand.

Study tip

By creating an argument and referring to key media ideas, such as symbiosis, you can substantiate the points that you want to make in a media essay. This demonstrates your attempt to evaluate media arguments.

Marketing

In order to succeed with the production and marketing of its content *The Radio 1 Breakfast Show* needs to publicise and promote its 'popularity', which is constantly under review as part of a non-profit-making institution. Marketing its brand to its audience is key to success. In today's segmented 'listening' market, programme managers must already know their target audience and the brand values of their shows. In this case, *The Radio 1 Breakfast Show* should attract and hold its audience's attention, through its energetic style and popular content, including the music and celebrity culture it promotes.

Corporate branding and promotion

Branding and promotion are conducted on the programme itself, for example through celebrity guests, movie reviews and entertainment news, along with familiarity with *The Breakfast Show* ident and stings. At the same time, the internet and social media offer opportunities for *The Radio 1 Breakfast Show* to provide a media image for the audio medium, for example through the use of iPlayer, *The Radio 1 Breakfast Show* website, Twitter, and related synergy with other radio features such as the BBC's Live Lounge or supporting Children in Need. In radio the most common demand made of marketing can be described as increased 'visibility', in recognition of the way audiences use radio in their everyday lives. Radio can be accessed while audiences are driving, by office workers during their working day and by web surfers while they are using the internet. And, with radio, due to technological convergence and mobile web connectivity, they may be able to respond to the programme immediately – an instant recognition of the media messages they receive.

Branding personality and radio idents

The Radio 1 Breakfast Show is embedded in the station ident and is a paramount unique selling point for the audience that leads to instant recognition of the brand. The show is reliant on the presenter's voice. The identity of the show is reinforced throughout by the use of jingles and station idents. For example, in Newsbeat the show has a distinct news broadcast that targets young audiences in its style and content (also true of the presentation of the Newsbeat website). Traditionally, news is not targeted at younger audiences and has often been packaged for adults.

To provide the audio equivalent of a product logo, radio requires presenters to use the station name in every link, along with station branding through a pre-recorded station identification, or a readily recognisable jingle or musical motif. This is evident in any content analysis of *The BBC Radio 1 Breakfast Show*, with its skilful use of music and sound effects throughout the show. This is termed 'image orchestration' (Keith, 1987) and communicates an image, slogan, feeling or emotion about the station to make the branded concept more memorable.

Off-air marketing

Radio also requires promotion of its programme content through off-air marketing. For the visualisation of its brand, for example, a simple internet search can locate:

- *The BBC Radio 1 Breakfast Show* website hosted by BBC iPlayer Radio.
  The features on this website include the BBC Radio 1 brand: a highly stylised, brightly coloured title. The website contains a 'listen live'

Branding The process involved in creating a unique name and image for a product or service.

Synergy The extended impact of sequential media messages delivered by multiple media forms and/or where audiences are exposed to a sequence of advertising messages from a single source idea.

Study tip

Making references to a range of examples from the set radio programme will enable you to achieve higher credit in media essays.

pop-up player and app. There are promotional still images of the presenter and past episodes to listen to. Other features include a playlist, podcasts, gallery features with schools events, and a clips page of embedded video interviews with celebrities and guests.

2 *The BBC Radio 1 Breakfast Show* Twitter feed: @R1Breakfast
https://twitter.com/R1Breakfast

This was in use while Nick Grimshaw presented the show and can still be located, but is no longer updated. The Twitter feed was aimed at a young online audience but constructed more like a blog or online diary than a regular Twitter feed. At its peak it had approximately half a million followers and displays the key promotional features of *The Radio 1 Breakfast Show*: recorded studio interviews, features on celebrity guests and partial live broadcast clips of the presenter working in the studio.

3 *BBC Radio 1 Breakfast Show* Facebook:
https://en-gb.facebook.com/R1Breakfast

Like the Twitter page, this is no longer updated but was in use during Nick Grimshaw's time as presenter. This is the official Facebook fan page for *The BBC Radio 1 Breakfast Show* and was used to post updates from the show and a few backstage extras as well as to gain audience ideas and comments for the radio! The Facebook page promotes an online community and features a plethora of publicity images of guests, including brief interviews, and promotional video trailers promoting the show. Its focus is to serve an online community and the ethos of the show.

4 *The BBC Radio 1 Breakfast Show* YouTube: www.youtube.com/user/bbcradio1

This features videos from *The BBC Radio 1 Breakfast Show*. It connects with audiences via the 'listen live' player on weekdays, or at any time via the BBC iPlayer Radio app. It supports the channel with its own playlists and hosts over 200 videos from the show with approximately half a million views. It offers much audience comment, video extracts and the ability to share video content. Radio 1 also has a Tumblr and a Vevo channel.

5 Radio 1 Instagram: @bbcradio1
www.instagram.com/bbcradio1/

This features photos and videos. It has been used by *The BBC Radio 1 Breakfast Show* as a gallery platform of publicity shots.

These internet sites work in a symbiotic relationship with the show to reflect changing audience practice in an online age. The challenges of marketing a radio programme have altered considerably since the 1980s and 1990s, when Radio 1 Roadshows (as live events) and merchandising promoted the unique brand identity and when raising awareness of this brand identity was considered enough to build a long-term relationship with the listener or fan.

In addition, the steady increase in the number of commercial stations competing for young listeners' attention (together with a greater number of digital services available via DAB, Freeview and Sky satellite receivers) has been mirrored in the growth in marketing expenditure and effort in the radio sector to market its content and services. For example, radio stations such as Capital FM and Heart are funded by advertisements played on air, which in turn affects the content and style of the programmes. Capital and Heart are owned by parent company Global, and are sister stations to Smooth FM and Classic FM. For their funding, all are subject to selling airspace to advertise companies, products and services on the high street or in the local area. As a result, the output of these stations is highly commercial, with chart and popular music dominating the schedules.

In the age of expansion for digital radio stations, greater choice leads to an increase in specialisation of each brand and the establishment of niches or segmented audiences. Every station has, to a greater or lesser degree, a target audience in mind, and marketing is now as much about differentiation as awareness. For the BBC this is about diversity, as indicated in the public service remit to which it adheres.

Technology

The broadcast output of *The BBC Radio 1 Breakfast Show* is complemented by an online presence with interactive features, including visual enhancements, that enable and encourage the audience to engage with the output and to share their views with both the station and other listeners. Radio 1 experiments with new technologies as they become available to ensure its young audience have the maximum opportunity to access programmes as and when they want. The show uses digital media for production, distribution and promotion, and social media accounts aid an interactive relationship with its audience.

Digital initiatives

Media institutions have been adapting their production strategies and output to fit the needs of **millennials**, a generation that tends to consume heavily and share content on the internet. Joe Harland, Head of Visual Radio for the BBC, has stated how Radio 1 aims to integrate online video in a bid to engage with the younger generation. For example, platforms such as YouTube and Twitter have helped BBC Radio 1 connect with its target audience of 15–24-year-olds.

This is one of the main reasons the BBC uses YouTube, alongside the fact that YouTube data is powerful enough to allow editors to see whom they are targeting, when viewers are watching, and for how long they are watching. Due to the immediacy and currency of media content, platforms like YouTube provide the BBC with free distribution of short video content, and as a media institution it has used digital initiatives to its advantage.

This rise in the visual imagery of radio is crucial in such a competitive online and global media environment. The idea behind sharing these entertaining clips and images is to encourage viewers to seek out the radio station itself. These visual images invite young audiences to co-opt into or be interactive with the broadcast of *The BBC Radio 1 Breakfast Show* through their abilities to watch, listen and share. According to the OCR Factsheet on *The BBC Radio 1 Breakfast Show*: 'Social media is one obvious way that the audience is interacting with the programme; even if most of this interaction is not "heard" within the programme itself, it shapes the nature of the programme and the involvement gains and keeps that audience.'

Knowledge check 13

Identify two internet platforms that *The BBC Radio 1 Breakfast Show* uses to visualise and market the show.

Millennials A term widely used to refer to 18–35-year-olds.

Study tip

It is important to use and show understanding of extensive media terminology in your media essays.

Media convergence

Media convergence is vital to media institutions and is a contemporary feature of media practice. In the online age *The BBC Radio 1 Breakfast Show* is developing towards media convergence, a characteristic that is apparent across all areas of the media.

'Media convergence' describes three phenomena:

1 How technology comes together as a single source due to digitalisation of content and platforms. For example, *The BBC Radio 1 Breakfast Show* is listened to on DAB, through the internet, on BBC iPlayer and so on. The advantage of this is being able to listen to media on a mobile device 24/7. Such flexible **time-shift** consumption has aided distribution and promoted *The BBC Radio 1 Breakfast Show*.

2 How media institutions diversify their interests and services to reflect a changing media environment. *The BBC Radio 1 Breakfast Show*'s symbiotic relationship with digital broadcasting illustrates this. The show has turned to platforms other than broadcasting to reach its audience segment. Distribution via other platforms, in particular the rise of internet-based interactive technologies, enables audiences to respond to the show and exchange content across several media.

3 A convergent culture where 'grassroots' activity (fans) meets corporate interests, 'blurring' the distinction between producer and consumer. The emergence of a participatory culture is evident in the BBC's remit for *The BBC Radio 1 Breakfast Show* and the young online audience that it aims to co-opt both into the show and into the values it embodies as a public service.

Media audiences

As has been stated, it is a prerequisite that the content of *The BBC Radio 1 Breakfast Show* not only meets the demands of the BBC's operating licence, but that this is justified through a commitment to a diversity of innovative and creative programming. In achieving this, the show appeals to a young media-savvy audience that is often under-represented by media institutions. It is also the share of this audience gained that matters, however, and this is measured by each programme's audience ratings. Despite year-on-year consistency in the BBC's share of the radio market, there was a gradual decline in listeners for *The BBC Radio 1 Breakfast Show* between 2016 and 2017, leading to much media speculation:

> **BBC Radio 1 posted a reach of 10.5 million listeners aged 10+ and *The BBC Radio 1 Breakfast Show with Nick Grimshaw* attracts 5.29 million listeners per week compared to 5.7 million in 2016.**
>
> (Source: OCR Media Studies Factsheet: *The BBC Radio 1 Breakfast Show* 2017)

Declining audiences?

Despite this decline in listeners, *The BBC Radio 1 Breakfast Show* consistently attracts young audiences with its programme style and content. It has had to cope with the transformation of radio in the online age. The scale and scope of available

Media convergence
The interconnection of information and communications technologies, computer networks and media content. It brings together the 'three Cs' – computing, communication and content – and is a direct consequence of the digitalisation of media content.

Time-shift In broadcasting, the recording of programming to a storage medium to be viewed or listened to after the live broadcasting, for example via BBC iPlayer.

Study tip

Using key facts and figures in the exam to support your ideas will illustrate your understanding of the content required.

music-streaming services and independent digital radio, along with a shift in **audience use and gratification** of the media, are contributing factors. Radio 1 is 'suffering' because its core audience is turning away from traditional listening. This is largely thanks to the arrival of streaming services like Spotify and Apple Music and online independent radio stations such as Last FM with its own free service-streaming websites and in-play radio stations.

RAJAR

The BBC Radio 1 Breakfast Show lost audience numbers between 2012 and 2018 throughout the time Nick Grimshaw presented it, but he had been brought in specially to develop larger audiences in the target age range of 15–29 and to shed the over-30s, a strategy implemented by Radio 1's controller Ben Cooper. Cooper stated that the station should not be judged solely on Radio Joint Audience Research (**RAJAR**) audience rating figures:

> You can't judge Radio 1 on RAJAR figures alone – just as you can't judge a newspaper solely on physical sales. You have to take into account our digital innovations as well. ... I'm pleased that Grimmy is doing what I've asked of him by keeping his young audience happy and scaring off the over-30s.

(Source: OCR Media Studies Factsheet: *The BBC Radio 1 Breakfast Show* 2017)

In fact, 90 per cent of the dip in Grimshaw's figures was from losing the over-30s. The show's use of social media and video content aimed to attract the target audience and, although the show had the lowest figures since RAJAR began, this reflects young people's media habits. A further source at Radio 1 said:

> Grimmy is the number one breakfast show in the UK for young audiences and that's all [the BBC] really care about. Teens are addicted to their phones so you can see why Radio 1 does so well on YouTube and Facebook.

(Source: OCR Media Studies Factsheet: *The BBC Radio 1 Breakfast Show* 2017)

Cooper went on to say that 'Radio 1 is evolving with its young audiences as we live through changing times for traditional radio, so it's particularly gratifying to see that in addition to around 10 million listeners, we have seen record figures for Radio 1 videos on Facebook with 80 million monthly views, and 1.4 billion total views on Radio 1's YouTube channel. As you can see, although traditional radio audience ratings exemplify a gradual decline in listeners, online media has raised the profile of BBC Radio 1 and the *Breakfast Show* in a different way.'

This change can be explained by the way in which media convergence of different platforms has transformed the audience. Institutions are no longer interested in keeping audiences together; instead they target different segments of the audience: for example Radio 1 targets a 15–29 audience segment whereas other BBC Radio stations target different segments. To attract young audiences across multiple platforms, media institutions trigger engagement. Audiences then take or exchange what they value and want to use of the content, often through the internet and social media networking.

The BBC Radio 1 Breakfast Show is a 50-year-old programme that has recently transitioned to the online **Web 2.0** digital environment. Traditional audiences may

Audience use and gratification An approach to understanding why, when and how people actively seek out specific media to satisfy specific needs.

RAJAR (Radio Joint Audience Research) The official body that categorises and measures radio audiences in the UK.

Knowledge check 14

What were the audience listening figures according to RAJAR for *The BBC Radio 1 Breakfast Show* in 2016 compared to 2017?

Study tip

It is important to show your understanding of how media institutions are coping with transformation in the digital age at the level of production, distribution and consumption.

Web 2.0 A second generation of the world wide web, which is focused on enabling people to collaborate and share information online.

be in decline, but for now *Radio 1 Breakfast*'s musical prowess and commitment to a public service make it as important as ever in the daily schedules of the nation. More importantly, the show represents an often under-represented social group across the media – 15–29-year-olds – providing them with a voice and presence in the online age and keeping to its commitment to make programmes for a wider spectrum of audiences and to offer diversity in a digital and commercial open market media world.

Summary

- Media institutions rely on the production of content and service provision. The BBC operates under a public service remit to protect it from commercial pressures.
- *The BBC Radio 1 Breakfast Show* under both Nick Grimshaw and current presenter Greg James provides content to its listeners that fulfils its public responsibility in the form of popular music and culture, which ultimately shapes the programme's style.
- *The BBC Radio 1 Breakfast Show* is an example of how the BBC as an institution fulfils this remit, serving the public as a non-commercial media institution.
- The show is produced with its young audiences at heart, through the provision of impartial, high quality and distinctive output and services that inform, educate and entertain.
- *The BBC Radio 1 Breakfast Show* has faced many challenges in recent years and, and as audience habits evolve, Radio 1 has sought to shift the emphasis away from solely traditional audience measurements to include digital platforms that better reflect how a young audience interacts with the show.
- BBC Radio has coped effectively with meeting its remit despite increased competition from the commercial sector and digital change, by modifying the show's content and style to make it distinctive in these ways:
  - Use of the presenter's celebrity status to appeal to the audience
  - Appeal to a younger segment of the radio audience
  - Adaptation to social media and use of the internet to visualise the brand to young people.

Practice question and sample answer: Radio

Explain how economic contexts influence radio production. Refer to *The BBC Radio 1 Breakfast Show* to support your points.

[15 marks]

e This question demands a response that demonstrates knowledge of the theoretical framework of media – that is, the nature of public service broadcasting. Display understanding of economic contexts and their influence on media products and processes, in this case audience engagement with the remit and the BBC's popular music policy. Avoid describing the BBC – evaluation questions are asking you to explain *why*. Aim to spend 25 minutes on this question.

Sample answer

Economic contexts influence radio production according to the nature of funding. *The BBC Radio 1 Breakfast Show* is funded by a licence fee under a public service remit. This remit is met if it remains popular with its target audience of under-30s and offers a diverse range of programme content, not only on the live shows but also via iPlayer Radio and YouTube for example.

Commercial radio stations are funded by advertising revenue generated by on- and off-air radio adverts. *The BBC Radio 1 Breakfast Show* lacks the radio advertising revenue available to, for example, the Capital FM Breakfast Show, but is instead funded by payment of a licence fee. *The BBC Radio 1 Breakfast Show* is currently the most listened-to show on Radio 1, forming part of Radio 1's overall public service broadcasting (PSB) remit to 'entertain, educate and inform', and is required to demonstrate a distinctive output of content compared to commercial radio.

The popularity of the show relies on the presenter to lead the nation's favourite breakfast programme in appealing to all teenagers. In contrast, Capital is owned by Global and is a sister station to Heart and Smooth FM, which are all funded by selling airspace to advertising companies. As a result, these stations are very commercial, with chart and popular music dominating their schedules.

The BBC Radio Breakfast Show is an example of how Radio 1 responds to the provision of a licence fee and targets a segment of the broadcast radio audience. By choosing a celebrity presenter and ensuring the show's style and commitment to popular and diverse music programming, it appeals strongly to under-30-year-old audiences. This is one way in which the BBC looks to justify its remit and licence fee payment to the public and politicians under its obligation to inform, educate and entertain.

e This student response is well-informed and demonstrates knowledge and understanding both of *The BBC Radio 1 Breakfast Show* and in addressing the question. It uses plenty of examples and contrasts public service with commercial radio economic contexts, especially through the issues of the licence fee and the public service remit. This is a comprehensive high-level response covering the relevant economic contexts and the role that *The BBC Radio 1 Breakfast Show* plays within these.

Video games
Minecraft

The specification requires you to study *Minecraft* as an example of video gaming. When discussing the production of a **video game** you will consider game design and construction, in particular of *Minecraft* as a game of creative play. You will then examine how *Minecraft*'s success is dependent upon how the distribution and game production is circulated online across a multiplicity of platforms and how it is marketed by the **users** themselves. Video games are a significant media industry and in 2016 the mobile gaming market was estimated to have taken $38 billion in revenues, compared to $6 billion for the console market and $33 billion for personal computer gaming.

Game features

Minecraft is a three-dimensional **sandbox game**, created and developed by Swedish-based Mojang Studios. It sets no specific goals for the player to accomplish, allowing users a large amount of freedom in choosing how to play the game. **Gameplay** is in the first-person perspective by default, but players do have the option to play in third person and there are different modes of play including *Story Mode* features. The game world is composed of rough 3D objects – mainly cubes and fluids – representing various materials such as dirt, stone, ores, tree trunks, water and lava. The core gameplay revolves around breaking and placing these objects. These blocks are arranged in a 3D grid, while players can move freely around the world. Players can mine blocks and then place them elsewhere, which allows for constructions to be built. The key characteristic of *Minecraft* as a video game is its creative and educational functions, which are more explicit in the gaming experience than in market-led rival games.

Video game All games played on a console, phone or tablet as an app or on a computer, that incorporate the essential component of gameplay: interactivity.

User A person who uses a computer or network service.

Sandbox game A game free of structure and constraint; players are free to roam and make choices about how they use the available content.

Gameplay The features of a video game.

Figure 1.6 In-game screenshot from *Minecraft* demonstrating the sandbox features

Minecraft has been described as a virtual world of Lego that involves following simple instructions in order to play: explore, mine and build. Users only have to log in and proceed to create a world full of textured 3D cubes. There are predominantly two game modes: Creative or Survival, although more recent additions include Adventure, Spectator and also multiplayer modes.

Independent media production

Markus 'Notch' Persson created *Minecraft* and developed the concept in 2009. He was inspired by several other games, such as *Dwarf Fortress*, *Dungeon Keeper* and *Infiniminer*. The latter had the most influence on *Minecraft* because it is **open-source software** and a multiplayer block-based sandbox building-and-digging game, in which the player is a miner searching for minerals by carving tunnels and through generating maps and building structures. *Infiniminer* also heavily influenced the style of gameplay, including the first-person aspect of the game, the 'blocky' visual style and the block-building fundamentals. Persson wanted *Minecraft* to have similar role-playing game elements, in which players assume the roles of characters in a fictional setting. Players take responsibility for acting out these roles within a narrative, either through literal acting or through a process of structured decision-making or character development. Actions taken within many games succeed or fail according to a formal system of rules and guidelines.

> **Open-source software (OSS)** Computer software with its source code made available; within its licence the copyright holder provides the rights to study, change and distribute the software to anyone and for any purpose.

Figure 1.7 Markus 'Notch' Persson, creator of *Minecraft*

'Video game production' refers to designing, developing and making a product for an intended market. Traditionally, video games are made by teams of developers for a production company and it is rare for an independent designer to take the risks involved in developing a game. Markus Persson is an example of such an independent producer developing a video game concept outside of mainstream media. The initial inspiration for *Minecraft* sprang from the fantasy role-playing genre of video games – a market that was already established. What Persson enabled was the development within the game of a role from a first-person perspective in a creative and imaginary way. His vision was made possible by allowing players to develop an identity through gameplay. Persson, as an independent producer, wanted the game kept for 'gamers' and as he developed the concept he tried to resist the temptation of large multinational gaming companies' takeover of the brand. This was quite unusual; in the gaming industry, it is more typical for products to be highly collaborative with many programmers working on a single project. This is demonstrated by the fact that whole studios usually receive either the praise or criticism for a newly-released game, as opposed to an individual.

Development

Minecraft is a story of the opportunities available to an independent games producer in the digital age. As an industry, video gaming has a 40-year history dating back to the earliest arcade games. It did not reach mainstream popularity until the 1970s and 1980s, however – this was when video arcade games and gaming consoles using joysticks, buttons and other controllers, along with graphics on computer screens, and home computer games were introduced. While the history of video games is not the focus here, it is important to be aware of post-millennium developments in gaming. Here are a few significant milestones reflecting the transformation of gaming technology:

- The first generation of **consoles** emerged, such as Microsoft Xbox. Some games had huge development budgets and cinematic graphics, for example for the Xbox 360 with high-definition video.
- The launch of the top-selling Wii console, with which the user could control game actions with real-life movement of the controller.
- The rise of casual PC games marketed to non-gamers and the emergence of **cloud computing** in video games. Online gaming and mobile games became major aspects of gaming culture.
- PC gaming has held a large market share in Asia and Europe for decades and continues to grow due to digital distribution.
- With the widespread consumer use of smartphones, mobile gaming has become a driving factor for games, reaching users formerly not interested in gaming or those unable to afford or support dedicated hardware such as video game consoles.

By 2011, with *Minecraft* being developed among the game community, Persson and his company, Mojang Studios, had a game concept with exponential global growth but without commercial backing from a mainstream publisher. The game's publicity relied on word-of-mouth recommendations between gamers – its users. For many media companies this would not typically have enabled growth or development of the concept. But, in the online age, Persson had the vision to circulate and generate the game via the internet and the video game community, so spreading the message virally about the game's value. This is a clear example of the power of collaboration.

Study tip

In identifying the independent producer of *Minecraft* you will be able to explain how a media product is created and developed from the perspective of the creator rather than that of a media institution.

Knowledge check 15

Name three influences on Persson's development of *Minecraft*.

Knowledge check 16

What is a sandbox game?

Console A specific device for playing video games.

Cloud computing Using a network of remote servers hosted on the internet to store, manage and process data, rather than using a local server or a personal computer.

Context

Social context: Online fan communities were important for the development and success of the game.

A consequence of this was that the **beta version** of the game had passed 'over one million purchases in just a month in January 2011, and by April 2011 Persson estimated that US$33 million of revenue had been made' (OCR Media Studies Factsheet: *Minecraft* 2017). Significantly, Persson's model is an example of a media concept that developed among a game community independently of the video game industry:

> In November 2011, prior to the game's official release, *Minecraft* had over 16 million registered users and 4 million purchases. Due to its popularity, *Minecraft* was released across multiple platforms, becoming a commercially viable franchise with increased interactivity. In particular, *Minecraft: Pocket Edition* was released on Sony Xperia Play, available on Sony Xperia smartphones. *Minecraft* also become available on Android and iOS devices shortly after.
>
> (Source: OCR Media Studies Factsheet: *Minecraft* 2017)

It was this ability to strike a franchise deal with an existing technology company, in this case Sony, to distribute the game that was a key feature of its success. This commercial deal helped secure *Minecraft*'s place in the video game market. Its significance was twofold:

- It was released on multiple platforms and increased audience interactivity.
- It was packaged as a game brand for a wider global audience and not just video gamers.

The rapid rise in *Minecraft*'s sales and popularity was a result of having identified markets among both existing game players and newer phone-savvy digital players:

> *Minecraft* has universal appeal. It is useful to explore how such a game can appeal to different ages, genders and audiences from different social and cultural backgrounds. The variety of different modes is certainly a contributing factor to the game's success, but also the way in which audiences can control and shape their own worlds and create new identities through mods [game modifications] and altering textures, maps and craft kits.
>
> (Source: OCR Media Studies Factsheet: *Minecraft* 2017)

Persson wanted to spread *Minecraft*'s concept and ethos within the control of genuine gamers. He also understood, however, that the game's success would grow with the backing of the technology companies, as they could provide him with the multiple digital platforms to distribute the game – ultimately to reach all the non-gamers now using mobile digital devices.

Beta version A version of a piece of software that is made available for testing, typically by a limited number of users outside the company that is developing it, before its general release.

Franchise A right to sell a company's products in a particular area using the company's name.

Study tip

It is important to use appropriate terminology throughout an essay and to apply this to the particular media area being studied. Video games have their own very specific and technical terminology.

Distribution

The development of *Minecraft* in 2011 occurred at a time when video gaming became 'online' and characterised by multi-gaming platforms. This was in part a response to gaming not just for consoles, but on any device. It also opened up opportunities for games distributors to connect to wider non-traditional gamers to game on media devices such as phones and tablets. This is evidenced by the advent of media convergence, which enabled digital distribution and global access to markets. This was exploited by Persson and Sony in the distribution and circulation of *Minecraft* in 2011.

It was at this point that *Minecraft* became a media product that could be packaged and distributed across multiple platforms to offer its users creativity via interactivity with its content and educational values, and with apparently limitless boundaries to its gaming.

> *Minecraft* is now a multi-platform game which is not only just for PC gamers but also those who own smartphones, Microsoft consoles (Xbox); PlayStation 3, 4 and PS Vita; and more recently Nintendo consoles (Wii U) and hand-held devices (Nintendo Switch and Nintendo New 3DS, New 2DS XL and New 3DS XL) – all of which opens up new markets of profitability and increased exposure to new and existing audiences.
>
> (Source: OCR Media Studies Factsheet: *Minecraft* 2017)

The progress of *Minecraft* after 2011 as a 'global' success is illustrated by this timeline:
- By 2012, *Minecraft* was available for Xbox 360 and Xbox Live.
- In 2013, *Minecraft: Pi Edition*, which was meant for educational purposes for novice programmers and players, was also released.
- In 2014, Microsoft acquired *Minecraft* intellectual property for $2.5 billion.
- In 2015, *Minecraft* reached 30 million copies sold. To date, over 121 official versions of the game have been created and sold across a variety of formats and platforms.
- By 2017, *Minecraft* was the second most successful video game of all time, behind *Tetris*, with over 100 million copies sold globally.

> **Knowledge check 17**
>
> Identify two advantages of distributing cross-media content.

Media takeover and merger

Minecraft, as a PC Java game, became a globally successful phenomenon across all consoles and hand-held devices. It is now a multi-platform game appealing to a wide range of users – not only PC gamers but those who own smartphones, tablets and other mobile devices. Mojang has struck deals with Nintendo, the largest game software seller, and Sony, as a hardware manufacturer and global conglomerate. By 2014 the **intellectual property rights** had been acquired by Microsoft, an American multinational technology company. This is not simply a case of the product being in the right place at the right time. These gaming giants and technology companies had a vision for *Minecraft* and how it could be distributed both globally and through its own gaming community. Their view was that beyond sales of hardware or software,

> **Intellectual property rights** The creation of rights to properties of the mind, including creative thoughts.

'gamers' could readily be sold add-ons and a whole range of merchandise, including *Minecraft: Official Magazine*, T-shirts, mugs, calendars, backpacks, hoodies, tie-ins with Lego, and *Minecraft* mini-games. Most recently a *Minecraft* movie has been proposed for 2019 (with Warner Bros. film studio). *Minecraft* has become a global brand with its own marketplace (its fans) to which to sell these offline commodities.

What should be clear is that after *Minecraft* became the property of Microsoft it cemented its position as a top-brand selling video game. When Microsoft bought Mojang and its intellectual property rights for $2.5 billion, the takeover enabled *Minecraft* to extend its reach further and secured its distribution to smaller mobile devices such as Xperia Play and to the Xbox Live marketplace. The exchange of the game and interactivity was made easier and not simply confined to gaming or PC consoles.

> **In a global context, the purchase of Mojang by Microsoft Studios for US$2.5 billion is a testament to the lucrative industry and global appeal of such a game across different platforms.**
>
> (Source: OCR Media Studies Factsheet: *Minecraft* 2017)

So, is it inevitable that independent media producers, such as Mojang, will be bought out by conglomerates like Microsoft? It does seem that in the history of the media there is a recognised pattern of diversification of interests by leading commercial companies in the takeover of independent producers – a pattern that has been long established in, for example, Hollywood film making.

Distribution enables the video game to be promoted to an audience and sold to maximise profits. The distribution of video games refers to all processes linked to delivering the media product to both physical and digital audiences, including cloud-based media and versions of *Minecraft* that can be purchased over the internet using such outlets as the PlayStation Network or Xbox Live Arcade. Recent additions include *Minecraft: Story Mode* available via Steam. Steam is a digital distribution platform developed by Valve Corporation that offers a digital rights management, multiplayer gaming, video streaming and social networking service. Steam can be considered the equivalent of an online video games store, comparable to iTunes or Amazon.

Video games consoles are an excellent example of a digitally convergent device, on which users can not only play games but can access social media, surf the internet, stream films and TV content, and upload content into cloud-based servers. Cross-media content helps maximise profits and also improves reach to new customers. This strategy for media consumption has developed as a business model in recent years, encouraging cross-play of video games across different platforms.

Marketing

The way that *Minecraft* has effectively managed and maximised its audience is the foundation of its success. Initially, Mojang relied upon word of mouth from its users and the online community of computer programmer and gamers. Since the Microsoft takeover, *Minecraft* has developed plenty of opportunities to market the brand and its gaming features. If a company buys the intellectual rights to a video game in a deal running into billions of dollars, then it expects a sizeable financial return.

Context

Social context: Consumerism has led to the development of *Minecraft* merchandise

---

Study tip

Use this debate on takeover in an essay to spark argument about the ideology of game developers and **prosumers**, who often surrender their creative licence to conglomerate interests to maximise profits.

Prosumer A consumer who becomes involved with designing or customising products for their own needs.

Knowledge check 18

What is the name of the production company that developed *Minecraft* and how much were the intellectual rights of the company bought for in 2014 by Microsoft?

Knowledge check 19

What is Steam?

Minecraft had originally debuted as a downloadable game with no money for its marketing budget. It had only five worlds for users to explore and was a single-player game. In 2011, *Minecraft* became a gaming giant because Persson built the game with his community. As he recalls:

> It's a weird way of making a game. You just put it out and keep working on it as you're making it ... I tried to make sure it's clear that 'This is not the game [that the buyers will see]. I'm just working on it, and you can play it while I'm making it.'
>
> (Source: http://observer.com, 14 March 2017)

He found, however, that his early adopters helped improve the game. Users reported bugs and, more importantly, created 'mods' (game modifications) that were new worlds, characters and items for gamers to play with inside *Minecraft*. The game's early community provided the initial growth and adoption through the power of collaboration and connecting with other users – filtering content and shaping the game's development.

Now that *Minecraft* has been subject to global success and management by its technology partners, it is sold as a leading video game brand. This is evident from a quick search of the internet in examples that both market and synergise the product. The *Minecraft* website (https://minecraft.net/en-us) enables the user to explore and buy the game's features. Under the main heading, the option to buy the product is prominent on the homepage. The website is the community location to download and explore realms and buy add-ons to the game.

The introduction of the Minecraft Realms service in 2013 was an attempt to give the producers more control over the distribution and circulation of the game. Realms are servers that are created specifically for players and are intended to keep players' *Minecraft* world online, accessible and safe to allow them to create, survive or compete. This invokes a sense of belonging, community and play amongst its users.

It is the establishment of a community within its marketplace that signals *Minecraft* as a lead video game.

Any successful media product requires a marketing strategy and, in the online age, a symbiotic relationship with social media. *Minecraft*'s Twitter feed (https://twitter.com/minecraft) exemplifies its highly developed use of online technology and has 1.8 million followers. Its banner is creatively and professionally animated. It is effectively a marketing platform for Mojang Studios, offering free giveaways, design information and what appears to be gaming advice to fans. With its highly commercial appearance, it represents a successful branding exercise for the game and company. Tweets frequently reference what is available in the *Minecraft* market and tie-ins with Microsoft consoles, with messages offering information such as behind the scenes previews about new products.

The *Minecraft* community then tweets brief replies in response to the development of concepts and technologies, creating awareness online of the products – which is exactly the aim of the *Minecraft* publicity machine.

Minecraft has also exploited the use of YouTube as a broadcast platform to promote its products, introducing game trailers and encouraging a video community willing to share its craft online. This prosumer community has aided online discussion of the game and improved viewers' abilities to play, create and share in it. *Minecraft* gamer celebrities have also emerged via YouTube, which in itself has attracted attention to the way the game is played and popularised it with online young, video-savvy media audiences. For example, reviews of games by popular YouTube vloggers such as PewDiePie are important for the future production of games as their feedback influences producers' thinking for future releases. This is exemplified in the game's survival mode, in tips on how to find food or how to stop the threat of creepers (exploding zombie-like creatures).

Minecraft Wiki (http://minecraft.wikia.com/wiki/Minecraft) is a free-to-use website referenced by *Minecraft* users to find out how to craft an item or realm in *Minecraft*. Users ask for help in the online forum. There is a history of the game's development on the site and a wide range of fans' feeds. This networked community of users exchanges ideas, finds free game resources and asks questions in relation to problem-solving and creativity. Away from established and recognised internet platforms, *Minecraft* reddit is a forum widely used and lists websites for add-ons and game features.

Educational value

In addition to the marketing and exchange of *Minecraft*, its educational worth is valued by users who create, play and share. This ethos is reflected in global projects and the educational value embedded in its program design. For example:

> **Minecraft has also been linked to non-profit projects such as the UN's Block by Block project, which encourages communities around the world to redesign their neighbourhoods using Minecraft. An educational version has also been developed, Minecraft Edu (2012), which has several applications to help teach subjects and develop a culture of computer programming among digital natives.**
>
> (Source: OCR Media Studies Factsheet: *Minecraft* 2017)

This cultural impact of *Minecraft* is significant in terms of creative and community use, with audiences sharing their own game modifications ('mods'), and game footage being made available across web forums and video-sharing sites such as YouTube. Different versions of *Minecraft* have been released to entice different audiences, moving away from creation-only narratives to include Story modes, spectator modes and multiplayer functionality across Minecraft Realms.

Audience participation has increased the appeal of *Minecraft* as users create new in-game content via beta-testing processes, producing shareable, downloadable mods, and texture and resource packs. Through this process the audience has

Context

Social context: These YouTube celebrities are an example of how the nature of celebrity has changed in the digital age.

become *Minecraft*'s biggest advertising and marketing campaign, promoting and sharing their modifications and ideas surrounding gameplay via YouTube and online forums. Users are craftspeople making and connecting the worlds they have created. Further developments include the introduction of a physical Lego set to engage younger audiences, as well as merchandise opportunities and bonus content for buying more than one version of the franchise across platforms – a cross-play feature (over different platforms) that has benefited *Minecraft* immensely.

The circulation and spread of *Minecraft* fan-made media across media platforms and dedicated fan sites, such as www.minecraftforum.net and blogs, means that there is an active and immersive community of gamers who share a common interest linked to *Minecraft*.

Audiences

On the basis of conventional video-game sales leader boards, with over 100 million copies sold across PC, mobile and console, *Minecraft* is a global product. Compare this to the video game *Grand Theft Auto V*, which has sold approximately 65 million copies. An investigation into the users of *Minecraft* in the 112 countries that register legal downloads of the game reveals that the USA, the UK and Canada have the most capacious appetite for *Minecraft* downloads. Countries in northern Europe, Japan and Australia constitute the remaining top ten. Microsoft reports that the game has been selling at an average pace of 53,000 copies a day since the start of 2016.

An age poll on Minecraft Forums (www.minecraftforum.net) states that the profile of the 86 per cent of players who were under 30 was made up of 20 per cent aged under 15, 44 per cent aged 15–21, and 22 per cent aged 22–30. Teenagers in North America and Europe seem to be the dominating **demographic**, with the majority of that demographic being male. This is reflected in the ethos and game design, which have particularly masculine characteristics in terms of constructing and creating.

What makes *Minecraft* popular with its audience is its multiple gameplay modes, which consist mainly of adding and mining a variety of different blocks in a digitally created world. *Minecraft* demonstrates through game interaction how audiences are not only making and connecting with other users, but are infinitely more creative through the use of the internet when compared with other game genres, such as the 'shooter' genre.

Minecraft also relies on audience interaction across games in order for the gamer to access an infinite world of craft and building. This is the key characteristic and asset of *Minecraft* as a sandbox game, which is immersive in its play in different realms and cultures. Users can create a digital world and invite fellow gamers, for example, in the Gardens of External Fall. It is in these realms that interactive play creates characters or mods, and modifications are created by the audience as an extra for the games that they are playing. It is this creative and interactive aspect of the game that engages *Minecraft*'s audience.

Creating mods has the feel of programming in the beta version of the game. It gives more options to the player to interact with the *Minecraft* world, changing the feel of it – indeed, *Minecraft*'s users see the game as thrilling and imaginative:

> **Study tip**
>
> Being able to reference your ideas and arguments about *Minecraft* users and writers provides a theoretical understanding to the topic of video games.

Demographic A particular sector of a population.

They add more settings and options to optimise speed, graphics or gameplay of the game. Mods are created from one player to another, such as memes, showing the creativity, the spreading of an idea. Texture packs are just one way in which the game could be fully transformed. They are the most spreaded mods, nearly every player has them. The texture packs completely change the graphics – they can have different themes such as Viking or Futuristic or even Mario.

(Source: OCR Media Studies Factsheet: *Minecraft* 2017)

Audience play and interaction is evident in its modding scenes, where 'users alter the gameplay mechanics, change the assets and develop new skins and textures for other fans of the game to use' (OCR Media Studies Factsheet: *Minecraft* 2017). This is then fed back to the game host and monitored through download numbers and audience reception online through social media. These modifications offer familiar pleasures to existing fans (narrative features, open world gameplay, and so on), along with new elements to target a wider audience (such as *Story Mode*). The creation of Minecraft Realms was a well-considered way to attract and encourage audiences to play the game on dedicated servers and so to increase subscription revenues. In these ways, audience interaction clearly affects the way in which the game is developed. *Minecraft's* uniqueness is established through the ability to use gamers as developers.

There exists an established network of fans across the internet who share game footage, tutorials, mods and hacks so that gamers can get new experiences from the game.

Fans on the Minecraft Marketplace site do not only trade different *Minecraft* products such as texture maps and learn new programming. The Marketplace is also a location where fans exchange ideas, and where the industry listens to fan ideas, sometimes enabling development that translates back into *Minecraft's* gameplay.

Summary

- *Minecraft* is an example of an originally independently produced video game that has grown exponentially in popularity and has since been taken over by an industry giant, Microsoft.
- The use of game modifications and the development of Story realms have created a unique game style based on building blocks – providing creativity and gaming for users.
- *Minecraft* now has a global audience and a mass market and the game is highly successful.
- The takeover by Microsoft enabled *Minecraft's* global distribution by the world's leading technology company, providing instant and online access to the game without the need for console-based technology.
- *Minecraft's* success since the takeover has been due to its ability to create and circulate engagement among its users – not just gaming fans but also non-traditional gamer audiences, such as apps players.
- The story of the success of *Minecraft* is not solely about its game features and production. Effective distribution, marketing and merchandising of the brand have created a video game for all gamers alike and has ensured that it has become one of the most significant and popular video games in recent times.

Practice question and sample answer: Video games

Evaluate how ongoing audience interaction influences the production of video games. Make specific reference to *Minecraft* in your answer. [15 marks]

ⓔ This question focuses on the influence of audience interaction on video games. You should avoid writing lengthy contextual introductions to the history of *Minecraft*, but recognise how the game's development was intertwined with how it was produced. Stay on-task and be succinct with the two or three main points that you want to make. Support your answer with examples and reference to your study of *Minecraft*. Aim to spend 25 minutes on this question.

Sample answer

Minecraft is a video game that could only have succeeded with audience interaction. When Markus Persson designed the game back in 2009 he was a gamer himself and his aim was to produce a video game that relied on the users creating, building and refreshing the game. This was the principle and ethos behind the video game. Its online community is able to advise and build *Minecraft*, and the company, Mojang Studios, takes on board its feedback in the on-going design of realms and by inviting a community of users to help develop the game through its beta programming.

Minecraft is premised on building blocks used like Lego, and it appeals to a young audience. Its fans like to swap ideas and comment on games as they develop their infinite *Minecraft* realm. In *Story Mode*, the game can develop as the user builds the world and this can be shared with invited friends. These modifications are not the only way in which the *Minecraft* community affects the game. Audience play and interaction is evident in its modding, where users can alter the gameplay mechanics, change the assets and develop new skins and textures for other fans of the game, so underpinning the ethos of the game to craft, mine and build. This creative gameplay is an appeal that differentiates *Minecraft* from other leading video game genres and gives it its universal appeal to both traditional and non-traditional video games audiences.

Minecraft is not only about adding better graphics and building realms; there are whole new games in *Minecraft*, such as *Ender Games* and *Minecraft Party*. These games are in a multiplayer mode, allowing the player to interact with others and to experience *Minecraft* in other ways. This principle of safe play was promoted and developed by *Minecraft* and is evident on its website.

Audience interaction is also promoted via social communities online through *Minecraft* fan forums and YouTube, where gamers such as PewDiePie are filmed playing the game. The company's successful production is reliant on audience participation and its creative nature made *Minecraft* the biggest-selling video game in 2017. It is the constant development of the game content and interaction in relation to its audience that informs the production of *Minecraft* and underlies its success.

e This answer provides an adequate application of knowledge and understanding of how audiences interact with video games and can be actively involved in their production, meeting Assessment Objective 2. It gives generally accurate explanation of how audience interaction has affected the production of video games and is supported by generally accurate reference to the set video game. The notion of audience interaction is exemplified through the gameplay features and explanation is offered of how audience interaction affects the production of the video game. This is a mid-level response.

Section B: Long-form Television Drama

Section B requires you to engage with the long-form TV drama. This can be in the context of the transformation of the form of traditional TV drama in an age of changing audience demands. You are required to apply academic ideas to the study of the long-form TV drama.

This section is weighted to be approximately 60 per cent of the exam and so equates to roughly 70 minutes' response time under timed conditions. (For an example of the question paper and mark scheme for Section B, please visit the OCR website.)

You will be rewarded for drawing together knowledge and understanding from your full course of study – be aware that the two set media products for Section B are to be studied in relation to all four areas of the theoretical framework and the contexts surrounding the media products. As a learner you will develop your understanding of the media through the consistent application of the four areas of the theoretical framework:

■ Media language: How the media communicate meanings through their forms, codes, conventions and techniques.
■ Media representations: How the media portray events, issues, individuals and social groups.
■ Media industries: How the media industries' processes of production, distribution and circulation affect media forms and platforms.
■ Media audiences: How media forms target, reach and address audiences, how audiences interpret and respond to them, and how members of audiences become producers themselves.

For Section B Long-form Television Drama, you will be asked to complete a comparative study of two contemporary long-form television dramas:

■ one from the set US long-form television drama list (List A)
■ one from the set European (non-English-language) long-form television drama list (List B).

Both long-form television drama lists are shown in the table below.

Table 2.1 The set US and European long-form television drama lists for Section B Long-form Television Drama

List A: set US (English-language) long-form television drama list	List B: set European (non-English-language) long-form television drama list
Mr. Robot (Season 1, Episode 1, June 2015), BBFC 15	*The Killing* (Season 1, Episode 1, October 2007), BBFC 15
House of Cards (Season 1, Episode 1, January 2013), BBFC 15	*Borgen* (Season 1, Episode 1, October 2010), BBFC 15
Homeland (Season 1, Episode 1, October 2011), BBFC 15	*Trapped* (Season 1, Episode 1, December 2015), BBFC 15
Stranger Things (Season 1, Episode 1, July 2016), BBFC 12	*Deutschland 83* (Season 1, Episode 1, October 2015), BBFC 15

> **Study tip**
>
> 'Comparative study' means drawing on skills you learned earlier in your course, for example detailed analysis, and contrasting elements of the two TV drama texts.

Your school or college will choose the most appropriate long-form television dramas for your study of this unit. You will need to spend time watching their selection from the above-named episodes. Be sure to cover all the areas of the media theoretical framework (including theory) in relation to your set episodes. For example:

- The influence of technological change, including digitally convergent media platforms, on the production, marketing, distribution and exhibition of long-form television drama in a global context (including the impacts of digital distribution platforms on the contemporary global television industry).
- How audiences consume and interpret long-form television dramas in different ways, including a consideration of demographic and technological factors related to consumption.
- How media language can be used to subvert or challenge genre conventions, and a consideration of other factors such as genre hybridity, intertextuality, multiple narrative strands and fandom.
- The media form-specific elements of media language that are used to create meaning, such as camera shots, angles, lighting, settings, locations, costumes, props, makeup, editing and sound.
- The values, attitudes and beliefs conveyed by representations and the social and cultural context of these.
- How representations may invoke discourse and ideologies and position audiences.
- How audiences' response to and interpretations of media representations reflect social and cultural circumstances.
- All relevant contexts, for example a consideration of the economic context behind the large budgets currently given to contemporary US long-form television dramas.

Question 3, the longer, comparative 30-mark question in Section B, requires you to connect or apply academic concepts to your study of long-form TV drama.

Question 4, the shorter 10-mark question in Section B, requires you to connect textual examples to a particular theory you have studied on the course.

Defining long-form television drama

Long-form television drama can be defined as visual media content characterised by in-depth, lengthy narratives. This form of TV drama story unfolds over approximately ten episodes, allowing for character and plot development. Susan Morrison in the journal *CineAction* states:

> **Long-form TV drama is a concept to describe the recent shift of interest towards television series of high quality drama that many consider to have replaced the cinema as a locus of serious entertainment. Unfolding over multiple episodes, hours, even years, these TV shows are seen to provide content, at times described as dark and difficult, yet produced in an innovative style that strains against the conventions of cinema, as well as network television. It now attracts some of the best and innovative writers and actors.**

(Source: http://questia.com, 2014)

Knowledge check 20

What percentage of the exam do the long-form television drama questions make up?

This description summarises this area of study aptly. Whichever long-form TV drama you are studying, you will discover innovation, often due to its director, writer and/or production team.

The inception of the long-form TV drama has placed emphasis on cinematic qualities and complex flexi-narratives. Flexi-narrative represents a complex storytelling form with these features:

- central characters whose motives develop with them
- a main storyline with interwoven subplots
- a combination of complex characters that are ambiguous or enigmatic, creating tension and questions for the audience.

Studying long-form TV drama will also enable you to examine cultural texts beyond the UK and to engage with more complex media representations and issues in a global media environment that genre-heavy UK drama does not address. Driven by distribution through internet platforms, such as Amazon Prime (distributor of *Mr. Robot*) and Netflix (distributor of *Stranger Things* and *House of Cards*), the growth of these web-based channels is proving considerable.

The long-form TV drama form has become accessible to online audiences who are no longer constrained by traditional media output or TV schedules. Time-shift recording, DVD box sets and opportunities for 'immediate' online consumption (often referred to as '**binge watching**') allow audiences more choice in how they watch TV drama. At the same time, production companies have freed themselves from the shackles of studio-based production and formulaic drama production.

In the USA TV is dominated by cable television such as HBO (launched in 1970) and many of the TV networks are subsidiaries of media conglomerates. In this institutional context, US network broadcasters must satisfy their advertisers by holding their market share. They are also controlled by federal regulation. The impact of this on their content is a reliance on highly formalised genre conventions and normative values that meet mainstream audience expectations – and generate cable-friendly, conservative drama. Through the four set US long-form TV drama texts, this section will explore how both online distributors (such as Netflix) and US cable TV stations (such as Showtime) are developing the form.

Binge watch To watch multiple episodes of a television programme in rapid succession, typically by means of box set DVDs or digital streaming.

Knowledge check 21

What is the definition of the long-form TV drama?

US English-language long-form television dramas
Mr. Robot Season 1, Episode 1, June 2015

Economic and social context

The first season of *Mr. Robot* premiered on USA Network, an American-based cable TV network, on 24 June 2015, and the episode title was 'hello friend'. *Mr. Robot* is shot on location in New York with a single camera set-up, and the running time for Episode 1 was 50 minutes. The production company is Universal Cable Productions and the distributor NBC Universal Television Distribution. The distribution of the episode was reliant on digitally convergent media platforms, which have transformed how the show is consumed by its audience. This model allows USA Network to first sell advertising on scheduled television channels and then to re-sell episodes through third parties.

Mr. Robot was distributed online via Amazon. Amazon.com is a technology company that is also the largest internet retailer, including of online media services. Amazon.com secured broadcasting rights in the United Kingdom, with the first season added on Amazon Prime on 16 October 2015.

Universal Studios Home Entertainment released the first season of *Mr. Robot* on DVD and Blu-ray on 12 January 2016. It contains all ten episodes, plus deleted scenes, a gag reel, a making-of featurette and **ultraviolet** digital copies of the episodes (allowing for time-shift viewing among online audiences and fans).

Distribution

Mr. Robot is an example of a US long-form TV drama that has been distributed on the internet. Thanks to Amazon's vast market reach, the drama's production company and director, Sam Esmail, was given the opportunity to send out the product to a global audience. The context for this has been the digitally convergent characteristics of online media, which have no national boundaries, unlike traditional broadcast media. Indeed, this model of distribution could even be seen as a threat to traditional broadcasters – as TV output has increased, more choice for online audiences means fewer viewers for cable TV. By opening up the market for US long-form TV drama in this way, more audience segments are exposed to the format in overseas markets.

The production of *Mr. Robot* remains within traditional TV production practice, and there are two production companies credited with the making of the drama: Universal Cable Productions and Anonymous Content. In addition, there were 16 global distributors, other than Amazon and its subsidiaries, and 13 other companies involved in sound, camera operation and settings. This signposts high-end production values for the making of *Mr. Robot*, and the size of the star-studded cast is further evidence of this. Relevant contexts of production, for example a consideration of the economic context behind the large budgets currently allocated to contemporary US long-form TV drama, suggest that *Mr. Robot* is a highly financed production.

Ultraviolet The industry standard digital code that enables the user to watch a programme on mobile and laptop devices.

Knowledge check 22

Which online retailer and technology company distributed *Mr. Robot*?

Study tip

The economic context of long-form TV drama production impacts on the style and form that the drama takes. Details of production costs and budgets are not always available, but you can reference 'high production values' to demonstrate the implied high budget of a show.

Patterns of ownership and control are significant economic factors in how the media operate and, characteristic of the international dominance of the American streaming services that distribute many US long-form TV dramas, *Mr. Robot* has had the backing of major cable studios. Media industries follow the normal capitalist pattern of increasing **concentration of ownership** into fewer and fewer hands, and the US TV drama sector is no different. As suggested by the theories of Curran and Seaton, this potentially leads to a narrowing of the range of opinions represented and to the pursuit of profit at the expense of quality or creativity. If this is the case, could *Mr. Robot*, as an example of a creative and innovative form, be possible only outside the normal constraints of broadcast TV? Could *Mr. Robot* have been created on traditional TV channels, given the controversial anti-establishment motifs in its narrative?

The producer's ability to negotiate a global deal with Amazon and other national distributors was made possible because of the heavily financed and arguably high quality cinematic-looking nature of this drama. Applying the theory of Hesmondhalgh draws attention to the issues of risk and profitability in long-form TV drama where high budgets are at stake, and producers try to minimise these risks by using formatting, for example by relying on trusted TV genres, the star system and co-production deals for the smaller European broadcasters. In the case of *Mr. Robot* the show had many outlets of distribution online, which cut the cost of using typical and costly TV networks and the risk of being constrained by the economics of cable television.

Audience

The growing consumption of the US long-form TV drama is evidenced in the swelling subscription for online platforms, such as Netflix and Amazon. Long-form TV drama is finding popularity among online audiences at a time when viral videos as a short video text have become ubiquitous through the development of YouTube as a free broadcasting platform. The popular and banal video form has a trending cultural value for global audiences when views of material can easily reach millions of hits. So the success and popularity of the long-form TV drama's significance is not only global but an indicator of the success of its form and content matter.

Long-form dramas are not aimed at traditional US cable TV audiences, partly due to their controversial topic matter. For example the anti-business motifs evident in *Mr. Robot* Episode 1 are not typical of the conservative drama found on cable television. You could argue that today's serialisation mode is very much on the consumer's terms, not the producer's, which changes the very nature of serialisation almost beyond recognition.

Realising growing demand for drama serialisation, *Mr. Robot* was launched on cable TV, which provided a window for audiences to engage with the drama. In the USA it attracted 1.7 million viewers, following a month-long cable campaign as a **windowing strategy** to promote Episode 1. Significantly, *Mr. Robot* was also promoted online as a pay-per-episode drama on Amazon Prime.

Concentration of ownership A process whereby fewer individuals or organisations control increasing shares of the media.

Study tip

It might be that some questions could be answered with explicit reference to a theory. For example, Baudrillard might be referenced when discussing *Mr. Robot*, but would be irrelevant when discussing *The Killing*.

Knowledge check 23

How many different global distributors did *Mr. Robot* have?

Windowing strategy A strategy used by producers and distributors to exploit their products. It involves segmenting global audiences by platform and territory, and rolling out television content across domestic and international markets through a series of sequential release windows.

The distribution and format does not influence the show's visual presentation as much as it inspires an action-packed plot: unlike a traditional TV series, the availability of the show after it is aired allows for so-called 'binge watching' where viewers can watch episodes end-on-end at their convenience and thus a dynamic storyline is essential to encourage this behaviour.

(Source: http://optimizethings.com)

The long-form TV drama is popular in its DVD form, and can also be watched as on-demand video and on video game consoles or laptop/tablet devices. The viewer is committed to a programme, sometimes for six or seven seasons. This means hours – hours and hours and hours – of invested viewing without the need to wait for weekly episodes. A characteristic of media audiences is to purchase whole series box sets for family entertainment, with online distributors and streaming services offering further provision online.

Audience breakdown

Mr. Robot appealed to crime thriller fans globally and online, and was aimed at young adult audiences. It has a **BBFC** 15 rating, meaning it has age-related content and is suitable for 15-year-olds and over to watch. As well as films for cinema release, the BBFC has a statutory requirement to classify videos, DVDs and some video games. The biggest challenge to such regulation is the content of online TV drama – as this must be dealt with more carefully than US cable TV to avoid harm.

To date, *Mr. Robot* is the only drama from the USA ever to have been nominated for and won the major drama award categories, including the Golden Globe Award for Best Television Series – Drama 2015, signifying critical acclaim and recognition from the industry for the quality of this TV drama. *Mr. Robot*'s critical reception draws attention to the range of different possible audience interpretations it evokes.

The media language

Mr. Robot communicates its complexity in plot development and characterisation through its style and form. It is a **polysemic text**, offering a multitude of opportunities for audience engagement or, as the theorist Hall argues, for the audience to 'decode' the text. If the act of reading becomes meaningful through the audience reception of a text, then this is most evident when viewing *Mr. Robot* at the level of negotiation of the text and its style.

Long-form TV drama enables viewers to engage with complex media representations and issues that genre-heavy UK drama does not address. *Mr. Robot* appeals to audiences interested in the genres of sci-fi and crime thriller. For Steve Neale, in his book *Genre and Hollywood* (1999), the recognisable familiarity of these genres and the narrative function of how the story is told in relation to the genre is a source of identification and pleasure for the audience of a media text. This is evident in the first episode of *Mr. Robot* being shot on location in New York – a setting that offers a representation of the diversity of urban America. The narrative is based on the character Elliot Alderson, who works at an American cyber-security company called Allsafe. This ironic name encourages the audience to negotiate with its meaning, raising the question 'Exactly how are our online lives safe?' Such features both invite audience interpretations of the text and hook them into watching the series.

BBFC (British Board of Film Classification) An independent organisation responsible for the national classification and censorship of films exhibited at cinemas and of video works, such as television programmes, released on physical media within the UK.

Polysemic text The idea that any text can have multiple meanings rather than a single meaning.

Study tip

Incorporating examples from the set episode and applying ideas from theoretical frameworks meaningfully to these will earn you marks in the exam.

The expectations of the narrative and broad sense of the thriller genre are set up in the opening episode:

- By day Elliot is a regular employee; by night he is a hacker.
- He leads a double life.
- He hacks details on social media and bank details.
- The client company ECorp suffers a 'hack' or breach of security.
- This breach is a plot by Mr. Robot, the leader of a fictional revolutionary movement, and he leaves a note for Elliot.
- fsociety represents a social group of hackers to which Elliot belongs.
- fsociety plans a digital revolution by deleting all debt records – a radical proposal and threat to corporate America.
- Elliot is invited to join fsociety's alternative cause. For example, in his first act of collaboration with fsociety, Elliot provides the FBI with an encrypted file falsely implicating ECorp's own chief technology officer as the orchestrator of the attack.

This set of narrative images reflects a number of audience expectations of what could happen in the episode. As the episode unfolds, audience expectations can be fulfilled or disrupted by innovation – in this case the presentation of the anti-hero in Elliot provides innovation in the storytelling.

Mr. Robot Episode 1 establishes an imbalance in a normal state of affairs – questioning the acknowledged role of cyber-technology firms as corporate businesses. Todorov's theoretical ideas on narratology can be applied to identify certain key elements in long-form TV drama – for example equilibrium (often implied) and disruption. Todorov's theory is helpful in teasing out the messages and values underlying a narrative and in pointing to the significance of the transformation between the initial equilibrium (displayed or implied) and the new equilibrium, for example in Episode 1 of *Mr. Robot* that of ECorp as a global tech company versus hackers.

Character-centred storytelling, as in *Mr. Robot*, constructs expectations within long-form TV drama. For example, Episode 1 clearly establishes characters and their spheres of action, which propels a compelling storyline. The episode is a testament to the blend of cinematic execution that has invaded linked-episodic narratives in recent years, and now combines with character-centred storytelling to define engaging storytelling. As a result of this *Mr. Robot* establishes a **narrative arc**.

A narrative arc is made up of the events in a story. A strong arc is vital if the form is to engage the audience from the start to the end of a long-form season and beyond. For example, *Mr. Robot* Episode 1 introduces the different and flexible narrative strands that will be developed:

1 Elliot represents an 'everyman' character, but the hero's journey is inverted. The tragedy-'hero tempted' motif.

2 He moves from protagonist to antagonist, representing the 'false hero' or the 'anti-hero'. Yet the audience remains sympathetic with the lead character.

3 The central importance of character, signposted by the use of voiceover in Episode 1, aids audience understanding and interaction with the text. This is Elliot's inner monologue, which keeps the episode feeling intimate and personal to the character.

Narrative arc An extended or continuing storyline in episodic storytelling media.

4   Episode 1 juxtaposes different and contemporary ideologies to inject more interrogative narrative drive, for example through the corporate 'them' versus hacker/'us' plots.

5   A signature POV (point of view) shot is used in every episode – this is not a traditional character-associated shot in TV drama.

It is not only the use of character functions and settings that are important to this long-form TV drama. Its cinematic qualities also act as visual signifiers in the storytelling. For example, the framing of the central character connotes his loneliness and social anxiety. This reinforces what Hall has termed a 'preferred reading' of the text: in this case that of Elliot as a central character who lacks conventional heroic attributes.

Representation and ideology

Mr. Robot is an American television drama series that is described as a psychological techno-thriller, directed by Sam Esmail. In writing the drama, Esmail consulted tech experts to give a realistic picture of hacking activities. Another influence was the Arab Spring (2010–11), where young people in North Africa who were angry at society used social media, including Facebook, to encourage a change in government and towards democracy. The praise by cyber-security firms for the technical accuracy of Esmail's direction has been noted extensively – adding to its realism and reflection of societal values.

Esmail drew on *Fight Club* (1999) as the inspiration for his main hacker character who suffers from a personality disorder, as well as for its anti-consumerist, anti-establishment and anti-capitalist viewpoints. Other inspiration for **intertextuality** in *Mr. Robot* includes:

- *Taxi Driver* (1976) for the narration by the protagonist
- *Blade Runner* (1982) for the character development
- the television series *Breaking Bad* (2008) for the story arc.

Intertextuality is a source of pleasure for the audience on the reading of a text – it provides generic familiarity and demonstrates how the long-form TV drama is building and developing upon previous media styles and conventions. Reflecting other important media texts also adds status to and signals the quality of the drama to producers and audiences.

Mr. Robot showcases some of the darker sides of technology and the power of big corporations, displaying the following themes:

- public fears of globalisation and corporate companies
- the instability of financial markets
- concerns over increasing dependence on technology
- the potential crisis of US identity and hegemony.

These representations invoke discourse and ideology that position audiences. In the reality of *Mr. Robot*, representation and ideology are combined to produce a socially acceptable and believable text about computers, hacking, corporations and American society.

> **Study tip**
>
> Watch the video clip on YouTube entitled 'Mr. Robot: The Art of Framing', about how *Mr. Robot* conveys loneliness with unconventional framing. Alternatively, search online for the video short on the cinematography of *Mr. Robot*.

Intertextuality The interrelationship between texts – the way that similar or related texts influence, reflect or differ from each other.

> Elliot is a social outsider who is positioned to challenge the system. As a hybrid detective drama, the plot favours meticulous details over special effects, with producers employing a career hacker to ensure that technology and Elliot's character are represented in a believable way. Everyone's personal information is available online through social media platforms and whatnot, and a brilliant hacker like Elliot has no trouble accessing that information at will.
>
> (Source: http://optimizethings.com)

Mr. Robot is a postmodern text in that it refuses any simple identification of 'the real' in the fictional world. It is supported in this by influences from *Fight Club* (1999) and *Blade Runner* (1982), themselves postmodern texts. It is a world where nothing is as it seems and nothing can be taken for granted. This is not just a description of Elliot's own paranoia, but rather of the actual objective features of the world that he – and by extension, we ourselves – inhabit.

The reality defined by the images and representations in *Mr. Robot* is a 'hyper reality', referencing a concept from Baudrillard. The images and story are simulations that challenge the truths of a society and posit alternative ideologies for the audience to engage with. Good media texts challenge the truth and the dominant discourse of society, and *Mr. Robot* enables the audience to inhabit the discourses of corporate America from a hacker's perspective. Thus, Episode 1 of *Mr. Robot* reflects the social and cultural contexts of America's technological society. The text presents a challenging set of themes and ideologies to be negotiated by the audience through complex layers of meaning. The richness and quality of such texts, focused on the way in which the story is revealed, is a strength of the long-form TV drama and turns this into a medium for serious subject matter and critique not usually found in commercial cable TV dramas.

House of Cards Season 1, Episode 1, January 2013

Episode 1 of *House of Cards* was directed by David Finche and was broadcast online by Netflix in January 2013. It was produced by the independent studio Media Studio Rights Capital (MRC), which purchased the rights to *House of Cards* with the intent to create an original Netflix series of episodes. Netflix reportedly agreed to contribute $100 million to the cost of producing the show for two seasons. Modi Wiczyk, MRC's co-chief executive, confirmed that 'Netflix won the right to distribute the series because it gave the creators total artistic freedom' (*LA Times*, 2013).

Production

House of Cards was pitched to several cable networks including HBO. Netflix was interested in launching its own original programming and outbid the networks. It produced and streamed the series for 26 episodes (two seasons). Netflix was the only bidder that was interested in purchasing the rights without seeing a completed pilot. As a result the show was not forced into the traditional programme structure, and this enabled its producers to manipulate story arcs introduced in episodes. They were not reliant on artificial **cliffhangers**, unlike UK soap opera (which is defined as a **continuing serial**), where shows scheduled on a regular basis throughout the year usually use cliffhangers to hook audiences to watch the next episode.

Study tip

When writing extended responses on the topic of the long-form TV drama, do evaluate issues relating to the study of the media. While there may be no right or wrong answer in the interpretation of a text, attempting to evaluate key media concepts will merit much credit in terms of marks.

Cliffhanger A narrative device that creates a dramatic and exciting ending to an episode and leaves the audience in suspense and anxious not to miss the next episode.

Continuing serial A TV serial with a continuing plot that unfolds sequentially, episode by episode.

While Netflix had previously ventured into original programming by greenlighting foreign shows that were new to US audiences, *House of Cards* represented the first show made for Netflix. It signposted Netflix's clear desire to be a producer of content and not simply a distributor of media products. This model could be seen as a threat to existing cable networks in the USA. *House of Cards* is a unique example of how long-form TV drama has developed, along with Netflix's strategy of the simultaneous online release of all 13 episodes of the first season. This strategy, initiated by an online technology company, illustrates the changing nature of media ownership and distribution.

House of Cards was broadcast with no commercial breaks or advertising, meaning it was not under the pressure that commercial broadcasters are to spread episodes over time to regularise and sustain the audience's attention. After all, in traditional and commercial broadcasting, advertising revenue pays for the programme.

> **The weekly release of episodes served at least two purposes: to fill airtime economically by spreading narratives out over time and, most important, to secure audience attention for advertisers on a regular basis ... The internet is attuning people to get what they want when they want it ... *House of Cards* is literally the first show for the on-demand generation.**
>
> (Source: *LA Times*, January 2013)

The simultaneous release of the whole season on Netflix generated an industry rethink of TV audiences. It led to a discussion of the way this made binge viewing possible at the click of a button. Audiences now control their instant gratification and this has made traditional TV schedules and their advertising outdated.

Audience

House of Cards provides an example of how the audience has changed in the online age. The online audience should not be measured as viewers in a traditional sense, but as **subscribers**. Attitudes to watching this example of the long-form TV drama illustrate the way in which the consumer subscribes to it in order to discuss it and share the content. Audience engagement with *House of Cards* highlights the need for producers to understand the reception of online dramas in more depth. It is a fascinating change to the environment of watching long-form TV drama, especially in adapting the way it is watched.

Netflix does not release audience viewing figures for its shows. It also does not organise audiences' viewing. Conventionally, TV flow and viewing has been managed by the cable broadcaster via its TV schedules. Netflix and *House of Cards* have viewers who subscribe, and this results in more freedom to watch and download according to individual choice. It has also meant that *House of Cards* had more freedom to develop and invest in the long-form TV drama, because the Netflix model meant there were not the constraints of building a brand or maintaining conservative programme content to deliver audiences to advertisers. Indeed, the opposite was true – the makers of *House of Cards* had creative freedom to produce a political thriller that could be creative, innovative and, to an extent, critical.

Netflix also offers something that cable networkers like HBO cannot: **asynchronous viewing** of a deep catalogue of programming – offering the audience total control

Study tip
Showing awareness of how a media institution, in this case Netflix, is evolving media practice demonstrates your ability to evaluate key issues.

Knowledge check 24
How many episodes of *House of Cards* were released simultaneously by Netflix?

Subscriber A person who has arranged by payment to receive or access a product or service.

Asynchronous viewing Viewing that does not happen at the same time.

over when and where they watch. This both challenges media theory and carries implications for how audiences consume media texts – and the effects of this, especially in relation to 'binge viewing'.

Gerbner's cultivation theory examines the long-term effects of television. The primary proposition of this theory is that the more time people spend 'living' in the television world, the more likely they are to believe that social reality aligns with the reality portrayed on television. But if the traditional TV audience is changing because of subscription channels, then the effect of these channels on new viewing patterns cannot be measured. This draws attention to the need to investigate the longer-term effects on individuals who consume long-form TV drama, especially heavy 'box set' users. The *House of Cards* audience is more male than female and, given the nature and tone of the programme, the typical interest in political thrillers and the payment set for subscription, potentially has the demographic of **ABC1**.

The biggest challenge for Netflix was how to create an episode of *House of Cards* that could be used to establish seriality when all the episodes are available at once. The seriality in narrative that functions within traditional TV drama also functions to maintain a revenue stream. Serialisation helps ensure that audiences tune in daily to advertisers' messages, and serials such as *The Sopranos* helped build HBO subscribers' loyalty.

It is Netflix's willingness to give the audience control over serial viewing that challenges assumptions that the best way to control programme costs is to stretch out episodes over time, measuring demand, and then to raise and lower advertising prices in response. Instead:

> Netflix will track viewership, not to adjust airtime prices for advertisers, but to measure subscriber demand and, it hopes, increase subscribers. Like HBO's move into original programming, Netflix's strategy is risky, but it is designed to attract subscribers to its streaming service – not necessarily to a particular programme.

(Source: http://blog.commarts.wisc.edu, 14 February 2013)

No doubt audience control of the pace of narrative consumption will affect social media communities. This strategy also challenges 'synchronous viewing as a business model, a model based on the limitations of legacy technologies rather than on some inherent quality of seriality ... Netflix's ability to expand offerings of commercial television programming will depend in part on its ability to keep attracting new subscribers. Offering viewers the option to binge, or to watch multiple episodes in a sitting, or to watch them over a longer time frame, may be Netflix's best bet for attracting new subscribers.' (http://blog.commarts.wisc.edu, ibid.).

Media language

The form and content of *House of Cards* is affected by the nature of its release and ownership. The result is that Episode 1 displays some challenging features. This is evident in the high production values of the opening scene – the presence of a star in the leading role and its cinematic look, similar to many long-form TV dramas focused on a complicated and highly stylised narrative.

ABC1 In media terms, an ABC1 audience is a demographic profile of an affluent media user, for example, defined by their social class (upper, middle and lower middle class). An educated audience.

Knowledge check 25

Who is the target audience suggested as the heavy box set viewers of *House of Cards*?

House of Cards also contains a highly complex character in Frank Underwood. The opening scene introduces him as he witnesses a car hitting a dog and then puts the animal out of its misery by suffocating it. As he does so, Frank explains to the audience his perspective as a politician: he is willing to do the unpleasant but necessary things – not only in reference to the dog, but also in politics.

House of Cards deploys unusual camera work and editing. The breaking of the **fourth wall** is characteristic of its visual style. It is unconventional for TV drama, but it is a device that allows exposition of the characters' motives. For example, Frank is centrally framed and dominant, speaking in the first person and revealing his ambition and desire for power, albeit with undertones of corruption. This mode of address emphasises the importance of the male politician.

House of Cards Episode 1 also establishes interweaving plotlines between politics, the media and personal relationships. An open episode structure encourages viewing of multiple episodes and higher viewer engagement, which is likely to lead to more subscriptions to the service. It is a political thriller, a genre not new to TV audiences, but one stylised differently to attract online audiences.

The drama is set in Washington DC, the USA's political capital. It uses a variety of domestic, political and business locations, for example the fictional *Washington Herald*. It is here that the audience is introduced to other main characters, including the newspaper's editor-in-chief and a journalist named Zoe Barnes. They are discussing what makes a good news story. The introduction of multiple plotlines becomes clear as the episode then cuts first to a fictional White House, where brief introductions are made to politicians and the audience are introduced to Frank's work setting and public responsibilities. Next, in dialogue with the character Linda Vasquez, the White House Chief of Staff, Frank reminds the audience of his help in the presidential election campaign. Vasquez tells Frank that Walker (the President) has given the post of Secretary of State to Michael Kern when it was promised to Frank. This lack of recognition for his support angers him and provides the motive for his plotting and retribution.

Political, social and cultural representation

Frank Underwood also plots with the press, revealing information on an exchange basis, thus reflecting a reality between politicians and the media. This representation is exemplified in the revelation that a congressman has been arrested for drink-driving and a false alibi has been created – setting up the theme of political scandal. The episode represents the media and the government as two opposing forces – with the media set on an exposé of the wrongdoing. This suggests the theme of corruption in public life as a preferred reading of the text. Full of political representation, *House of Cards* implicates the audience in creating its meaning and power, in deciding who are key influencers within the episode and its storytelling. This drama has the scope, creative freedom and budget to be realistic and accurate enough for the audience to believe in it. We see 'power' represented not only in its typical political settings, but also in its domestic settings and themes. For example, in marriage, Frank and his wife, Claire, are represented as stronger than any single individual and as a 'power couple' – typically a reference to people with a certain position of power and authority. It is through such stereotypes that the audience is encouraged to negotiate meanings in this text.

Fourth wall A performance convention in which an invisible 'wall' exists between the actor and the audience. When an actor 'speaks' to camera, they are said to be 'breaking the fourth wall'.

Study tip

You will not need to analyse set episodes textually, but do make reference to selected examples of the long-form TV drama when you address the question.

House of Cards Episode 1 also interweaves the themes of the male politician and the female reporter. Zoe Barnes is a professional journalist. She contrasts with Claire who is defined by being Frank's wife – a part of a couple. Critically, this assumes that relationships with males ultimately have the most importance in women's lives, a feature of what Van Zoonen describes as a **patriarchal** society. Zoe Barnes contrasts with this as a journalist introduced in Episode 1 while debating 'what is a good news story' with her editor, which can be read as an attempt to break with traditional feminine typecasting in the media. Her representation can also be read as negative, however – she is childlike:

> She often is shown in a childlike manner. She dresses like a college student, wearing hoodies, T-shirts and jeans to the newsroom; very short, very tight dresses at events; and sweatpants and a sweatshirt in her apartment ... further, she typically is shot from a high angle, which accentuates her short and slight frame, and she often is depicted filling only a small portion of the screen.

(Source: Chad Painter, 'Gender games', *Journalism Practice*, 2017)

Patriarchal Relating to or denoting a system of society or government controlled by men.

Figure 2.1 Frank Underwood with journalist Zoe Barnes in *House of Cards*

Zoe's character and her actions can be interpreted as unprofessional and unethical – she does a deal with Frank Underwood, who feeds her news stories. This raises her profile while letting him push his agenda through the press. These stories are important, with wide-ranging implications for the direction of the nation. The representation of women in Episode 1 needs to be understood in relation to Frank's actions, as women are represented as serving his needs. As Van Zoonen's concepts of the representation of women in the media suggest, gender is performative – our ideas of femininity and masculinity are constructed in the performances of these roles.

Study tip

Always be sure to apply theory. Do not simply cite it!

Homeland Season 1, Episode 1, October 2011

Production, social and political context

The series was developed by Showtime, a premium cable and satellite television network that is the flagship service of the Showtime Networks subsidiary of CBS Corporation. Showtime features blockbuster movies, first-run feature films, stand-up comedy specials and documentaries. The channel also carries original series, with newer episodes primarily being shown on Sunday and Monday evenings. *Homeland* is produced by Fox 21 Television Studios. The first season won the 2011 Golden Globe Award for Best Television Series – Drama, signposting the critical acclaim the series received.

Homeland is an American spy thriller with the storyline revolving around two central characters: Carrie Mathison, a CIA officer with bipolar disorder, and Nicholas Brody, an American sniper and sergeant for the Marine Corps, who is found at the start of the episode having been missing in action, presumed dead. Mathison comes to believe that Brody, who was held by al Qaeda as a prisoner of war, has been turned while in captivity, and that he poses a threat to the USA. The series focuses on a storyline that evolves from this premise, together with Mathison's covert work as an intelligence agent.

The title *Homeland* refers to a post-9/11 America that is focused on the threat of terrorist activity at home as much as abroad, and where political violence is widely felt to be required to curb that threat. In context, 'homeland security' is an American umbrella term referring to the national effort to prevent terrorist attacks within the United States and to minimise any attacks that do occur.

From its initial broadcast, *Homeland* also raises a debate with its audience on the moral legitimacy of political espionage. The narrative complexity deployed in *Homeland* follows a narrative arc, conventional to the long-form TV drama, around two characters: Mathison's role as an intelligence officer and Brody's return to the USA as war hero. The plot twists of *Homeland* are comparable to the successful cable TV show *24* with its themes of loyalty and legitimacy, and demonstrates the established convention of these elements within the crime/political/espionage thriller genre.

From the outset in Episode 1, the narrative plotting of *Homeland* examines the shifts in allegiance, suspenseful revelations and plot twists that the medium is particularly able to deliver. The centrality of Mathison's role in the storytelling is a hallmark of the different way in which long-form TV drama narrates a story, in this case through the perspective of a strong female lead. As they have developed, the elements of homeland security (on network television, at least) have come to rely on particular models of heroism, as well as on themes of terrorism, trauma and violence.

Distribution

The original broadcast of the opening episode, called 'Pilot', was on 2 October 2011 and received just over 1 million viewers, becoming Showtime's highest-rated drama premiere in eight years and drawing record-setting audiences for the cable network. The first episode was made available online more than two weeks before the

Study tip

In the study of US long-form TV drama, it is necessary to understand the social, economic and political contexts of the drama and its storytelling. For *Homeland* these relate to national security and the terror attacks the USA has suffered post-9/11.

television broadcast, with viewers having to complete game tasks to gain access to the episode. Episode 1 received a total of 2.78 million viewers inclusive of additional broadcasts and on demand views. In the UK the first season performed well on Channel 4, where it attracted approximately 2.8 million viewers. *Homeland* was also distributed in Canada, Ireland, India and Pakistan as significant overseas markets for the drama.

Television **video on demand** (VOD) systems can either stream content through a set-top box device, allowing viewing in real time, or download it to a device such as a computer. Showtime as a cable TV-based television provider offers both VOD streaming and free content, whereby a user buys or selects a movie or television programme to play on a television set or via the internet. *Homeland* is a good example of how a successful cable TV show has been distributed as video on demand using digitally convergent devices, and it illustrates how the internet provides a wider and global reach to online audiences.

Video on demand
Systems that allow users to select and watch/listen to programmes when they choose to, rather than having to watch at a specific broadcast time.

Gender representation

Homeland is a layered, polysemic text that enables and triggers engagement with audience readings in relation to gender and the crime/political thriller genre. This is evident in the first episode as Mathison suspects the would-be war hero Brody has been turned by a terrorist group. This storyline is presented in the lengthy dialogue that Mathison has with Saul Berenson, her mentor at the CIA. The series also created controversy over its content and themes, being analysed as both a critique of US foreign policy and an affirmation of the need for national security, set as it is after the terrorist attacks of 11 September 2001. It carried undertones and reflections that aimed to support the Obama administration's foreign and domestic surveillance operations.

Knowledge check 26

How many viewers did *Homeland* receive in the UK for its first season?

The text positions a strong female lead character, thus challenging the expectation of a male lead conventional to more conservative US TV drama. This ploy can be attributed as a success to the writers of *Homeland* coupled with the cable TV company Showtime, already renowned for network dramas that aimed at a female audience by 'picking up on representations of women that are virtually invisible in popular media' (Andrea Press, *Women Watching TV*, 1991). The network's basic cable programmes in the United States seem to have proliferated around and grown from the success of Mathison's complex female characterisation. The question of what female-centred television looks like in the period of *Homeland*'s success is a complex one, with evidence of exciting new representations and character developments.

The central female character, Carrie Mathison, appears to be a vehicle for working through cultural shifts in the relationships between government, politics and private life. For example, in the opening episode the audience is introduced to her as a consummate problem-solver in the public arenas of politics and national security. Indeed, it could be argued that Episode 1 allows the audience to negotiate the deliberate use of anti-stereotypes of femininity. An effective strategy used in *Homeland* is to go inside the stereotype and open it up from within to deconstruct the work of representation – which is what the opening episode invites the audience to do with Mathison. At the same time, Mathison also deals with her own illness (a reliance on an anti-psychotic drug) and behaviour in a personal life that is represented by picking up men without 'relationship ties' while she 'swigs' alcohol, declaring to her male companion, 'I'm ready to go now'. Judith Butler's feminist theory applies to Mathison's gender performance throughout the episode: she is foregrounded in her actions as a woman despite the masculine traits that audiences might associate these actions with (such as her picking up men). The representation of women through Mathison presents their bodies and minds for display, challenging stereotypes of femininity and reinforcing characters with masculine traits.

The centrality of the female character highlights Carrie Mathison's lead role in the national security of the USA but, at the same time, shows her to be a rule breaker, for example when she illegally orders phone taps and surveillance in Nick Brody's home. In Episode 1 she is constructed in the role of the **voyeur** – traditionally a masculine activity – looking at, or in this case spying on, Brody's home and his personal and family relationships. It is unusual to see a female character with this power to 'look', but it defines her willingness to find information by any means necessary.

Voyeur A person with a general interest in spying on other people's private activities or moments.

Another dimension of Mathison's character is her mental illness and extreme emotionalism. Her prowess as an intelligence officer is often represented as contingent on her illness, as suggested by the discovery in the aspirin bottle of pills that are not aspirin. It is her actions rather than her appearance that define her as the lead intelligence officer – her perseverance in the line of duty. For *Homeland*'s Mathison, her illness (she is on a drug called clozapine) manifests in obsessive attention to detail; examples are the background wall on Brody that she has in her house, which is organised in meticulous detail, or her exchange with Virgil her co-worker in the surveillance van. By her own admission Mathison admits, 'I am crazy … I have a mood disorder.'

Mathison is an over-emotional character – angry and in search of the truth – but she is loyal to the cause of national security:

> Carrie Mathison prominently features in Episode 1 with an ability to crumple her face and quiver her lip in intense distress that foregrounds this emotionalism with extremely wide-open eyes and gestures like raking her hand through messy hair that express frustration with her inability to fully protect the US Homeland.
>
> (Source: Diane Negra and Jorie Lagerwey, 'Analyzing *Homeland*', *Cinema Journal*, 2015)

Mathison's personality disorder becomes a strength and adds complexity to her character when it helps her realise that Brody is using his finger movements while on live television to give a coded message (a clue triggered psychologically from watching a jazz band on her date night). Taking this information to Saul, her CIA mentor, allows the dramatic plot to unravel.

Figure 2.2 Carrie Mathison and her Brody investigation wall in *Homeland*

For the audience, and for the programme makers, *Homeland*'s ideological significance lies in its skilful discussion of ongoing debates about the security of American life. With its female-centric view, however, the series also emphatically rebuts the dominant and presumptive masculinity of quality crime TV. As significant to the audience is the way the series breaks with the more masculine address that seems to go along with this genre within the conventions of a long-form TV drama. For example, Nick Brody's reunion with his family is emotional in a melodramatic scene at the airport, which is to be expected after an eight-year separation. Brody's masculinity is again represented differently – he is a war hero, but a war hero with sensibilities, illustrated by him comforting his wife, Jessica, when she is distressed at discovering his scars from torture.

The representation of family life is another significant element at the heart of Episode 1 – the absent father returns to what is apparently a broken family, reinforcing the importance of family values. In fact, this is a cover for his past actions. The audience is privileged to glimpse the truth of events in the Middle East when, in a flashback sequence, Brody beats an American soldier under Abu Nazir's command. The paradox of such revelations is the essence of the spy/espionage genre – the audience questions whether Brody will be caught out and, if so, how.

Homeland is ultimately described by its production team as a political **melodrama**, and Episode 1 both introduces and reinforces Carrie Mathison as the series' lynchpin, the female who will be proactive in revealing the truth behind the 'war hero' storyline.

Homeland reinterprets many long-established aspects of the crime genre, via an effective female investigator character and a complex form of narration that obscures motives and delays resolution. For example, in the scene at the CIA's headquarters at Langley, there is a debrief of Nick Brody by senior intelligence officers. Mathison interrogates Brody's account of his captivity, cross-examining him over the legitimacy and paradoxes in his account of meeting Abu Nazir and thus providing the audience with further narrative hooks for subsequent episodes.

Melodrama A sensational drama with exaggerated characters and exciting events; often overemotional.

It can be argued, however, that *Homeland* atypically acknowledges a political landscape that works within, rather than against, the broader context of the crime thriller/espionage drama in relation to national security. This is shown, for example, by the sheer number of covert spy operations that litter the storyline – such as the spying on Brody in the park from the back of a van, which introduces another flashback that privileges the audience with the information that Brody is lying about the death of another soldier, but not for what reason.

Stranger Things Season 1, Episode 1, July 2016

The first episode of *Stranger Things*, written and directed by the Duffer Brothers, was streamed on Netflix in July 2016. All eight episodes were released in the summer and were potentially aimed at younger online audiences – a more traditional release time for this genre would be in the autumn, around Halloween. The series was produced by 21 Laps and released as an original Netflix series, Netflix having sole distribution rights.

Audience

Stranger Things is a long-form TV drama marketed by a successful online campaign employing traditional film marketing techniques, that is, promoting genre, stars, writers, and so on, using new media technology. The marketing of the series relied on word of mouth and the following methods to make its release visible to Netflix's online subscribers and to a targeted range of viewers:

- a four-hour live stream on the Twitch app, which is popular with video gamers, promoted with gamers playing games in the studio build of the *Stranger Things* basement
- a cinematic trailer released on YouTube
- the first eight minutes of Episode 1 used as a spoiler on YouTube
- an interactive virtual reality 360° video of the basement set
- dedicated Twitter, Facebook and Instagram accounts with features linked to a Q&A about the series, interviews and other content
- widespread sharing of video memes and gifs online, promoting a fan community who are '**textual poachers**' wishing to use these products to create their own culture, for example via fan sites.

This extensive marketing of *Stranger Things* is evidence of how US long-form TV drama has substantial financing and the backing of TV production companies and online technology companies looking to distribute the product to a global audience via the internet. Netflix's strategy for marketing *Stranger Things* needs to be understood in relation to the drama's style and form, in particular its use of intertextuality, its ability to trigger engagement with its audience and, as theorist Henry Jenkins would argue, its ability to connect with its fans.

Knowledge check 27

What genre of media text is *Homeland*?

Textual poaching The appropriation by fans of media texts or the characters within them for the fans' own pleasure.

Intertextuality

Set in the 1980s, *Stranger Things* makes plenty of intertextual references to a range of texts from this era, such as Stephen King novels and the fantasy game *Dungeons and Dragons* – the game being played in the opening scene. The drama makes reference to past films, Steven Spielberg's *E.T. the Extra-Terrestrial* (1982) for example, with the camera panning down from the sky emulating the opening of *E.T.* What connects these different cultural texts are the genres of horror and science fiction. This connection or reference to genre in Episode 1 of *Stranger Things* provides familiarity and a starting point for audience interest and engagement.

In part, the success of *Stranger Things* is due to the narrative pacing of its events. The Duffer Brothers made successful movies in Hollywood, but the biggest challenge for them of working with long-form TV drama was how to tell a cinematic story over eight hours rather than two. The Duffer Brothers understood the demands of traditional cable and of satisfying advertisers with continuous narrative hooks to retain their audience on a daily and weekly scheduled basis. Netflix allowed the Duffer Brothers flexibility to tell their story because its method of streaming and distribution removed the pressures of cable TV. Hearsay, rather than fact, says that the production costs for *Stranger Things* were low, but we do know that the casting of two stars, Winona Ryder and Matthew Modine, added status to the show, which was received well by its audiences. A succinct opinion is offered in this *Guardian* review of Episode 1:

> **Stranger Things is fun for almost all the family, depending on your juvenile cohorts' response to occasional gory scenes. The pace is (just about) fast enough to keep younger viewers hooked, and anyone old enough to remember 1983 for real is in for a richly enjoyable retro-feast whose cockle-warming abilities make up for (what is for us) a slightly predictable narrative.**
>
> (Source: *The Guardian*, 12 July 2016)

Episode 1 of *Stranger Things* allowed the drama to introduce character and setting within the era of 1980s America – stylising them with a sense of nostalgia for both older and younger audiences. For example, the opening sequence, of the disappearance of Will Byers and his encounter with the creature, toys with the idea of a mysterious creature that can consume humans. This plot also sets up a sense of genre – the use of a monster provides familiarity for the audience, referencing the scifi/horror genres. This playfulness with genre is evident in *Stranger Things*, as although it is like a teen movie (set around a group of children and a school community), it is also serious and scary, dealing with children's sensibilities.

Genre and narrative

It might seem that, as soon as the monster is introduced, the Duffer Brothers are committed to telling a horror narrative and therefore to abandoning in-depth characterisation. But Episode 1 of *Stranger Things* defies this and enables the writers to establish setting, character, genre and motif within a crime drama context as well. For example, the day after the disappearance of Will Byers, the writers

Knowledge check 28

Which 1982 Steven Spielberg movie is referenced in the opening scene to *Stranger Things*, and how?

Knowledge check 29

What is an intertextual reference?

introduce the community and questions are raised about Will's whereabouts – but not straightforwardly, for example questioning Will's father, Lonnie Byers, on his involvement in his disappearance.

Rather than plot an immediate response to the disappearance of Will, the episode then cuts to a scene at Hawkins National Laboratory. A team of scientists, including Dr Brenner, put on protective suits before entering a quarantined underground subsystem. There, they find a strange biologic growth spreading – originating from a mysterious fracture in the wall.

This exemplifies the flexi-narrative used in the episode – with different strands of the story plotted in the laboratory, the high school and in Benny's Burgers, where a girl with a shaven head appears and steals burgers. The plot is interwoven as the story of the community unfolds and at the same time introduces a range of characters. This interweaving of the narrative is important for long-form TV drama because its serialisation provides the audience with multiple entry points to the text and means the story can be told over a period of time.

The cinematic look and detail to set design are important for producers and audiences of the long-form TV drama. In *Stranger Things* this is an eclectic mix of horror meets teen movie that appeals to the audience, as does the ability to get to know the characters on a weekly basis. For example, introducing the monster early in the narrative helps the programme makers set up the seven further episodes and gives them time to build characterisation and develop the narrative. The Duffer Brothers also play with narrative devices and the characters. For example, in a flashback scene, Joyce is in the woods at Castle Byers ready to surprise Will with tickets to see *Poltergeist* – a reference to a Steven Spielberg horror movie from 1982.

In his study of genre, Steve Neale recognises the importance of **intertextual relay** in media texts in generating extra generic functions. This is evident in how *Stranger Things* was marketed as a long-form TV drama, requiring an intertextual relay of pre-publicity and reviews to attract large audiences. For example, the font used for the series title has connotations of sci-fi/horror and the posters invoke memories of a *Star Wars* film poster. Drawing on familiar audience expectations, these devices helped define and circulate the narrative image of *Stranger Things*.

A characteristic of long-form TV drama narrative devices is the use of time-lapse scenes, which are used to provide key moments of disorientation (disrupting the chronology of events) and to inject a more 'interrogative' narrative drive. Episode 1 of *Stranger Things* introduces a range of storylines that are crime-led. For example, a scene with the character Benny and his girlfriend is interrupted when a woman claiming to be from Social Services arrives to collect the girl. Benny invites the woman into the diner, and when his back is turned she shoots him. Benny lies dead on the floor while a number of agents arrive to collect the girl. She uses her telekinetic abilities to kill two of the agents and then escapes. This latter ploy adds to the narrative layers of the episode and establishes yet another **narrative enigma** for the audience.

> **Study tip**
>
> Do use elements of the episode summaries from the TV dramas as examples in your response as this will add detail to your argument, exemplifying your knowledge of the programme content.

Intertextual relay Genre codes and conventions established not just in media products but also in products that refer to or promote these products, such as critical writings, advertising and marketing material.

Narrative enigma A narrative code that entices the audience to watch the rest of the media text as they are curious about why things are not as they seem and what will happen next.

Figure 2.3 Promotional material for *Stranger Things* illustrating intertextual relay

Stranger Things presents its setting of the American community darkly: an apparently normal community is attacked by aliens and the plot thickens as a murder takes place. Yet its appeal as a long-form drama is the flexible nature of its narrative (that is, its multiple forms). Multiple narrative strands, however, are just one of many important conventions in long-form television drama, including genre familiarity and characterisation. It is these that enable Netflix and the Duffer Brothers to make quality content for online audiences. *Stranger Things*, like *House of Cards* (also produced by Netflix), feels like a big movie in that major plotlines are completed, delivering audience satisfaction, but enough is left unresolved to indicate there is a bigger and continuing story to tell, as narrative threads are left dangling purposefully at the end of a season.

Audience and fandom

Henry Jenkins investigates the ability of media users to construct meaning via communications among fans – a form of spreadable media. Jenkins sees the act of media consumers spreading content as active not passive. He believes that audiences play a crucial role in the dissemination of media products in the online age and states, 'If it doesn't spread, it's dead.'

- Jenkins believes that this sharing is an act of participation and categorises it as collective intelligence.
- He explains that this act leads on to deeper levels of participation; the initial sharing can be described as 'preparing to participate'.

■ He describes media products that provide audiences with deeper layers of engagement as doing so not just to attract the maximum number of viewers but also to retain the audience for longer and engage them in more meaningful ways.

This concept of spreadability is evident in the marketing of *Stranger Things* – it is aimed at young online audiences and film fans who are most likely to explore new technologies and a convergent media culture, for example video gamers. For Jason Mittel, spreadable media seem to pull the audience in the direction of engagement due to the narrative complexity of storytelling, especially in television form:

> **The opposition between spreadable and drillable shouldn't be thought of as a hierarchy, but rather as opposing vectors of cultural engagement. Spreadable media encourage horizontal ripples, accumulating eyeballs without necessarily encouraging more long-term engagement. Drillable media typically engage far fewer people, but occupy more of their time and energies in a vertical descent into a text's complexities.**

(Source: http://mediacommons.futureofthebook.org, 25 February 2009)

Nostalgia has had a part to play in the targeting of the audience for *Stranger Things* through its intertextual reference of the 1980s for its visual style – the *mise-en-scene* of the drama appeals to fans. In addition, the narrative arc is very similar in formula to teen horror stories of that period, for example the *Friday the 13th* films.

It is the fact that *Stranger Things* created a strong online fan base, a community that shared a collective interest in its stylisation, that produced its success. The Duffer Brothers worked with a successful cinematic genre, were playful with its visual style and combined this with the mode of media used for TV long-form drama. It was the fans' negotiated readings of the text that then created discourse around its subject matter and characters – asking if it was a teen show, a horror story or a sci-fi drama that was being set up in the first episode. As 'textual poachers', the online audience produced their own readings of the text, also leading to prosumer texts being created online to parody the series and circulate the series itself among the audience. This in turn caused a demand for fan merchandise – opening up opportunities for Netflix of the kind that traditional media companies like Disney have enjoyed for years.

While *Stranger Things* did a great job of taking its audience back to the 1980s, it was via very twenty-first century means that they expressed their love for it, first across social media and then by creating fan sites – a 1980s-style computer game and title sequence generator being two examples – and *Stranger Things*-themed gatherings. The cast have also taken to social media to share behind-the-scenes treats and photos.

The success of *Stranger Things* as a long-form TV drama lies in its storytelling, but also in the way it employs nostalgia in this process, both as a narrative device and in its visual style. This, combined with Netflix's release strategy and the chances taken to connect with and engage fans and online audiences, propelled *Stranger Things* to its success as a US long-form TV drama, demonstrating the variety of this type of drama and the quality to which it can be produced for global TV audiences.

Study tip

Remember that you will be comparing different US and European long-form TV dramas in your exam response, but this does not stop you from using a range of examples from within the form.

Knowledge check 30

Which media theorist identifies spreadability as a fan-based activity?

European non-English-language long-form television dramas
The Killing Season 1, Episode 1, October 2007
Economic, social and political contexts

The Killing is a Danish crime thriller series created by Søren Sveistrup and co-produced by DR (the Danish Broadcasting Corporation) and ZDF Enterprises, which hold international distribution rights. *The Killing* Episode 1 was first broadcast on the Danish national television channel DR1 in 2007, and has since been transmitted in many other countries worldwide through ZDF Enterprises.

In the book *Beyond the Bridge*, Tobias Hochscherf and Heidi Philipsen argue that the last ten years have seen a golden age of Danish television drama and recognise both the long-form TV drama and *The Killing* (2007–12) as a prime example of this. The Danish drama series was shown on BBC Four in the UK, attracting more viewers in the UK than its US counterpart *Mad Men*. The regular audience figures in Denmark were 1.7 million and in the UK were approximately 500,000 viewers per episode. *The Killing* exemplifies the popularity and success of Danish television drama and demonstrates that first-class TV drama can be produced in Europe. *The Killing* also illustrates the quality of long-form TV drama that has been produced in recent years under DR's public service remit. This remit, which was established in 1925, has principles similar to those of the BBC in the UK.

The Killing has had global success, but it spread particularly throughout Europe (including the UK), Australia, South America and Asia. It proved particularly attractive to middle-class viewers in the UK, and indeed it helped establish a special Saturday slot on BBC Four for subtitled foreign dramas. *The Killing* was so successful as a global product that it inspired an American remake produced by Fox 21 Television Studios for the US domestic market, which Netflix globally distributed in 2014. As well as its successful viewing figures and global reach, *The Killing* won awards for best international drama series including at the BAFTAs in 2011.

At the centre of the narrative of Episode 1 of *The Killing* is Detective Chief Inspector Sarah Lund. A notable characteristic of the drama is that each episode (in all three seasons) represents a single day in the police murder investigation – it is essentially a 'whodunnit' narrative. Such elongated story-telling allows for detailed exploration of the emotional reaction of the victim's family and friends to a horrific killing, something not often presented in TV crime drama. Sarah Lund is represented as petite, feminine and charming; a female detective wearing signature jeans and sweaters while she investigates a brutal killing.

Figure 2.4 Sarah Lund in *The Killing*

The Killing Episode 1 is also a prime example of European long-form TV drama produced under and grown out of a strong public service remit. This shares the conventions of the commercial form but is also concerned with wider social, political and moral issues. *The Killing* was described as 'Nordic Noir' as a way of defining its stylistic and narrative elements, and this term was subsequently used as a brand for Danish drama abroad. *The Killing* employs a visual style that relies on open, forlorn spaces where it is often cloudy or raining, and interior shots with muted lighting and monochrome colour design, creating a distinctive look to the drama.

The Killing Episode 1, set in the Danish capital city Copenhagen, is filmed as a crime drama with elements of family drama and melodrama overlaid. This hybrid mix was intended by the creators to attract both male and female audiences. Episode 1 presents different perspectives on the crime with a narrative that unfolds at a slow pace to reflect the case's daily progress in each episode. Each 50-minute episode covers 24 hours of the investigation, with the first series consisting of a lengthy 20 episodes – confirming *The Killing*'s categorisation as a European long-form TV drama. It also reveals the economic context of a small publicly owned national broadcaster that can finance just one long-form drama per season, and this is achievable only in co-operation with other European television producers. Indeed, only four to five per cent of Danish drama is financed by the Danish public service licence fee. DVD box set sales and a number of international co-producers (the BBC among them) and distribution and co-operation agreements have aided the global success of Danish dramas, including *The Killing*. By 2013 Danish drama had become very popular as content on multiplatform online media, such as Netflix, itself recognition of the quality and significance of Danish TV drama.

Knowledge check 31

What were the audience figures for *The Killing* in Denmark and the UK respectively?

The language of Danish TV drama

The series is noted for its plot twists and dark tone and for giving equal emphasis to the stories of the victim's family and the effect in political circles of the murder and police investigation. Here is a succinct synopsis of the first episode:

> It is Detective Chief Inspector Sarah Lund's last day with the Copenhagen police force; she is about to move to Sweden to join her fiancé and transfer to Swedish police. Everything changes when 19-year-old Nanna Birk Larsen is found raped and brutally murdered. Sarah heads the investigation and is teamed up with her replacement, Detective Inspector Jan Meyer. Troels Hartmann, a male politician, is in the midst of a hard-fought mayoral campaign when evidence links him to the murder. The girl's family and friends struggle to cope with their loss.

(Source: adapted from Wikipedia)

The title sequence to Episode 1 of *The Killing* shows a girl running through a wood. Its cinematic style **connotes** suspense, making the viewer wonder who is running and why. It is shot with **key fill lighting** – making it feel dark and eerie. The female character is being followed by a killer and audience expectations of and familiarity with the crime genre are established in first long shot, then in a sequence of mid shots as the killer chases the victim. **Non-diegetic** music adds suspense to the scene. The opening scene is interspersed with images of fingerprints, further signifiers of a crime scene investigation, thus anchoring the genre of this TV drama.

In Episode 1, the audience is introduced to Sarah Lund as she is woken at 6:30 a.m. in her family home. This scene is slow-paced. After receiving a phone call she arrives at a cordoned-off crime scene. Very early on, it is evident that not much daylight is used and it is raining and gloomy, matching the sombre tone and atmosphere the producers wish to convey. The body of the victim is found in a field near the woods, a **signifier** of the open forlorn space used in the drama. The victim's clothing is also found and provides a police lead on the crime upon the discovery of a video membership card. The plotting of the investigation into the crime is interwoven with Sarah Lund's last days in her job before she leaves for a new life in Sweden.

This dialogue-laden TV drama is reliant on conventional **shot-reverse shots** between characters to provide slow-paced continuity and to set up the crime storyline. The episode also establishes narratives around different characters, such as the businessman Theis and his company Birk Larsens – the name on the video rental card found at the crime scene. *The Killing* Episode 1 also interweaves political storylines around a forthcoming mayoral election and important Danish social issues, including family and child care, refuse collection and education. The storyline of the crime's suspect unravels as Sarah Lund questions the victim's stepmother at Birk Larsens and the audience are positioned to understand that police inquiries are being made into where the missing girl Nanna (Theis's daughter) is.

In part due to its commitment to a public service remit, Danish TV drama consciously incorporates into its storytelling a cause-and-effect narrative, covering in this case crime and broader socio-political contexts. It is the nature of Danish TV drama to weave intricate characters and plots that converge and diversify to encourage audience

While this unit does not require textual analysis of the drama episode, you may need to offer a synopsis and understanding of the text supported by examples from the episode you have studied.

Connote To suggest or imply meaning beyond a literal or principal meaning.

Key fill lighting The use of lighting in a set-up where elements of the *mise-en-scène* have been filled with stark or contrasting lighting.

Non-diegetic Not a part of the real world of the text, for example added music that creates ambient sound.

Signifier A sign's physical form (the term 'sign' in semiotics denotes an object, setting or event that indicates meaning).

Shot-reverse shot A film technique where one character is shown looking at another character (often off-screen), and then the other character is shown looking back at the first character.

interpretation and readings of events. This linking of compelling storytelling to relevant discourses in society is described as double storytelling. It layers a text with meaning about Danish society, and also primes the show to appeal to international markets.

Representation and audience

The Killing is good crime drama, but its producers also use the genre as a vehicle to promote **discourse** on moral, political and social problems. For example, *The Killing* contains specifically Danish representations – of rivalry with Sweden and of the nature of Danish local politics. Crime narrative is proven to have a global cultural resonance and, in this case, it helps sell Danish TV drama abroad. The transparency effect – that is, the packaging of a global and American style of storytelling – blended with the motifs of public service storylines creates what is known as transnational infotainment drama. For Tobias Hochscherf and Heidi Philipsen in *Beyond the Bridge*, *The Killing* is an exploration of how one incident impacts on different layers of society, from a whole school to the career of one politician.

The episode also reflects socially contested gender relations – the police management and sparring politicians are male, reinforcing patriarchal power, but the narrative follows the agency of a female protagonist, whose professionalism and efficacy is foregrounded by her male colleague Jan Meyer's boyishness and willingness to give up. There is similar ambiguity in gender representation in the victim's parents Theis and Pernille: they are presented as equal partners in their business and family affairs, but, stereotypically, it is the husband who goes out to search for the missing girl while the wife stays at home. Episode 1 also reflects two separate worlds – that of family life and that of politics – within the same society, the former with values of caring, solidarity and authenticity, the latter with values of competition, spin politics (with its underhand point-scoring) and conspiracy. The series requires some understanding of Danish local politics.

Audiences were co-opted to *The Killing* via the internet as a way of encouraging interaction with this long-form TV drama. Its website was used to identify and develop fans' five fictional relationships with Sarah Lund. Other ways the internet was used to encourage interaction included:

- a dedicated website set up in Denmark for audiences to cast their opinions on who might be the prime suspect
- a blog featured in *The Guardian* newspaper in the UK to document each episode as it progressed.

The programme makers recognised that the internet provided opportunities for making strong links between the fictional character and the show's audience. The website for *The Killing* generated online activity and interaction between the drama and the audience. Henry Jenkins professes that such participation allows elaboration and collaboration in deciphering narrative enigmas in the text – loose ends can be pieced together as fans generate engagement with the text. The website for *The Killing* encouraged users or the fan community to interact with the 'whodunnit' storyline.

The audience is also invited into the urban landscape of Danish society, as signified by the aerial shots of the rooftops of Copenhagen in Episode 1. This world and the reality that is constructed invites viewers into the socio-political life of the drama.

Study tip

When making reference to drama extracts, identifying elements such as editing and shot-reverse shots as post-production techniques demonstrates correct application of media terminology.

Discourse A general term for a number of approaches to analysing written, vocal or sign language use, or any significant semiotic event.

Thus interest in the Danish way of life was transposed to a global perspective through the representation of place and culture.

Borgen Season 1, Episode 1, October 2010

Borgen is a Danish political drama created by Adam Price and produced by DR, the Danish public broadcaster. It is set in Copenhagen and focuses on Birgitte Nyborg, who is elected as the first female prime minister of Denmark. Episode 1 is entitled 'Decency in the Middle'.

The programme has also been broadcast in various regions outside Denmark, including in the USA, the UK and other European countries. In the UK, the first season was aired on BBC Four in 2012. BBC Four is a channel dedicated to delivering content on education in the arts and regularly acquires and broadcasts European long-form TV drama. The purchasing of Danish TV dramas such as *Borgen* has proved very successful in achieving the channel's aim of delivering alternative drama programming from a global perspective.

Social and political context

With 1.67 million viewers, a 64 per cent Danish TV audience market share, *Borgen* headed the Danish TV drama list of most popular TV dramas. It has been sold to 60 countries globally. The drama's success can also be measured by it winning awards for international best drama in Italy and at the BAFTAs in 2012.

Like *The Killing*, *Borgen* was shown during the prime-time slot on Sunday evenings on DR1, the state television main public service broadcaster. Episode 1 reflects the show's economic and production context of a small publicly owned national broadcaster that has limited finances but a successful track record in selling series internationally, thus encouraging co-operation with other European television producers. This led to the creation of a very national product but with international appeal.

The drama was produced with the same underlying principles as *The Killing*:
- It had a focus on complex lead characters.
- Its narrative was based on the theme of politics and the media, encouraging discussion and engagement with the socio-political context of Danish society, for example an open discussion of democracy and citizenship.

Borgen translates into the Danish word for 'castle' and refers to Christiansborg Palace, which is a castle in Copenhagen and the location of the Danish Parliament, establishing the political motifs and narrative. Episode 1 begins with a cultural reference and epigraph: 'A prince should have no other aim or thought but war and its organisation and discipline', from Machiavelli's *The Prince*. This political citation signals **cultural capital** to the audience, inviting them to apply its meaning to what follows on screen.

Borgen was shot with cinematic influences with a high budget look; it was shot mostly in a TV studio with opulent sets and long establishing shots of the city and parliament. It is also characterised by long sequences of dialogue-laden drama, frequent framed medium two-shots and **walk-and-talk scenes**. This style is also often used in US long-form dramas – something of an influence on Danish TV drama productions.

Knowledge check 32

Identify one way in which audiences were invited to engage online with the TV drama series *The Killing*.

Cultural capital The social assets of a person (education, intellect, style of speech and dress, and so on).

Walk-and-talk scene Where the camera tracks the actions of the characters; often used for mini-plot summaries.

The drama deals with the complexity of Danish politics, illustrated in the title sequence, for example, by an interesting montage of black-and-white and sepia images cut with both interior and exterior shots of the Danish Parliament. A TV newsroom also dominates the images, along with key figures including a woman kissing a child (representing the themes of the media and family life). The title sequence is stylistically conventional of TV drama titles, signposting the dramatic through the use of orchestrated music and silhouetted images of character and place, capturing the mood of the political drama.

This opening sequence intercuts between political interviews and a television news editor's office. Opposing politicians are being interviewed: one about the coalition of Danish parties; the other on taking a firm political stance towards asylum seekers from the Middle East. *Borgen* also focuses on the private lives of these politicians, with atypical representations of the trials and jubilations of being a politician in Denmark, juggling different political viewpoints in their domestic and public life. The Danish drama establishes a fictional tale about democracy and power relations in the public sphere – that of a civil democratic society that now faces the challenges of being online. For media theorist Manuel Castells, these are three messages and debates that take place in the contemporary global public sphere that is largely dependent on the global/local communication media system:

> **This media system includes television, radio and the print press, as well as a variety of multimedia and communications systems, among which the internet and horizontal networks of communication now play a decisive role.**
>
> (Source: Manuel Castells, 'The new public sphere', *Annals of the Academy of American Political and Social Science*, 2008)

In the past, discussion of politics in Denmark occurred in the media through documentaries and news broadcasting. *Borgen* explores how these themes are discussed at three different levels: in what way they reflect on Danish politics, how they are presented by the media, and how they affect individual citizens and families.

Representation

Borgen has similarities with *House of Cards* and *The West Wing*, both US political dramas that conduct a discussion of politics from different critical perspectives. *House of Cards* reflects with scepticism on politics, through the character Frank Underwood; *The West Wing*, as an exposé of White House politics, brings investigative engagement with the audience to long-form TV drama. *Borgen* Episode 1 sets out to hook the audience into the world of Danish politics using the conventional structure of the long-form TV drama.

The drama's political storylines interweave around the central character Birgitte Nyborg after her landslide election victory. The main plot focuses on how her family life becomes enmeshed with her role as Prime Minister and asks whether she can deal effectively with the evolving political crisis concerning asylum seeking. This situation impacts on her family – her supportive husband and their two children.

Knowledge check 33

What is the name of the Danish public service broadcaster?

Among other central characters are her **spin doctor**, Kasper Juul, and up-and-coming journalist and anchorwoman Katrine Fonsmark. Birgitte is a polyphonic character driven both by her relationship with and love for her family and by her role as a politician. She is portrayed as an admirable character whose traits are complex yet ethical and honest; she tries to serve her country as best she can. Birgitte's narrative arc is woven in with the plots of Juul and Fonsmark. Their character interaction via breaking news brings their storylines together.

Episode 1 can also be seen to reflect contested gender relations through these various representations of the impact of feminism on patriarchal society:

- Politics and the media are shown to be mostly male-dominated.
- Women are represented as skilled professionals, such as journalists.
- Birgitte is represented as powerful and decisive.
- Many representations reflect the work of constructing femininity, especially via Birgitte and via Katrine as a journalist and TV anchor. Both characters emphasise the performative nature of femininity – Judith Butler's feminist theory – where the performance of gender is foregrounded through representations of women preparing to present their bodies for display, here in the worlds of politics and the media.
- Lars Hesselboe's wife fits the traditional patriarchal stereotype of the 'hysterical' woman, for example on a shopping trip with her husband when she declares publicly, 'You never treat me!'
- Masculinity is represented positively from a female perspective, for example the ultra-supportive husband Phillip who has compromised his own career for five years.
- Danish family life is at the heart of the drama, reinforcing family values.

Political representations include:

- Denmark being represented as a multicultural society
- Laugerson's attack on asylum-seekers being portrayed as a social problem
- depiction of consensual decision-making and coalition politics of a left-wing government in Denmark
- the welfare state in Danish society.

Such gendered and political representations are a part of the narrative strategy of *Borgen*. It is not just a political and gendered drama but, like *The Killing*, it upholds its public service remit through the content and motifs of the drama – which it also successfully sells to a global audience. According to Tobias Hochscherf and Heidi Philipsen in comment on Danish TV station DR:

> We are a public service broadcaster. We have to be just as entertaining as commercial competitors but at the same time we need to have a social political dimension in our serials.

(Source: Tobias Hochscherf and Heidi Philipsen, *Beyond the Bridge*, 2016)

Borgen is an agenda-setting drama, promoting political debate and reflection upon a civilised society. It is through the motifs of public affairs that the programme makers have essentially packaged Danish politics into the long-form TV drama. This may be seen not only as a representation of a national culture but as part of a globalised ideology of western liberalism. There is a cynical view of spin-driven politics, yet it provides an optimistic vision of democratic politics in a European country.

Spin doctor A spokesperson employed to give a favourable interpretation of events to the media, especially on behalf of a political party.

Knowledge check 34

Which theorist can be applied in relation to feminist readings of gender in *Borgen*?

Trapped Season 1, Episode 1, December 2015

Economic context and distribution

Trapped is an Icelandic television series created by Baltasar Kormákur and produced by RVK Studios. RVK (http://rvkstudios.is) produces films and television including *Trapped*, which has been distributed globally and received critical acclaim and audience ratings. It is seen as an international success and possibly RVK Studios' biggest hit yet. After its screening at the Toronto International Film Festival in 2015 it was broadcast on RÚV, the Icelandic national public broadcasting service. RÚV was launched in 1930 and currently broadcasts a variety of general programming to a wide national audience via two radio channels and one television channel.

Trapped has been sold to numerous broadcasters around the world, including to the BBC, which began screening the long-form TV drama in February 2016. The Weinstein Company, a **mini-major** US film studio, purchased the US distribution rights. *Trapped* is the most expensive television series ever made in Iceland, with its one series estimated at 1 billion króna (£7 million). Before this, Icelandic television series rarely exceeded production costs of 100–200 million króna (£1.5 million), and *Trapped*'s much larger budget signified an improving set of production values as well as levels of investment in Icelandic TV drama. This is exemplified by the high-quality design of the title sequence and the original musical score, along with the cinematic shots of the landscape and the scale of the first episode.

Mini-major A film studio that, while smaller than the major studios, tries to compete directly with them.

Trapped was first aired on RÚV on 27 December 2015, and broadcasting rights have since been sold to several countries. It first aired on BBC Four in the United Kingdom and has been broadcast across Europe, in Australia and the USA. It has been described by academics as a White Noir drama because of its Icelandic landscapes where it is consistently snowing and its presentation of the beautifully bleak main setting – the port of Seyðisfjörður, a remote coastal town in eastern Iceland. The other location used in the drama is Reykjavik, Iceland's capital city.

> **Study tip**
>
> While it is important to learn the domestic institutional contexts of European long-form TV drama productions, it is also worth understanding the different organisations and production companies that produce them in a global context.

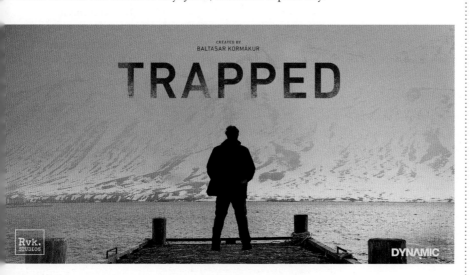

Figure 2.5 Andri Ólafsson in the bleak Icelandic setting in *Trapped*

Social and cultural context

Trapped is a crime drama. Series 1 has ten episodes; in Episode 1 a small town in a deep Icelandic fjord has been snowed in. Body parts are discovered by a fishing vessel and the local police discover a dismembered body and suspect murder. They believe the body has come from an inbound ferry from Denmark. As the ferry is seized in port, the suspected killers flee into a snow blizzard that isolates the town – the ferry is geographically entrapped by the weather and environment. Andri Ólafsson, the local chief of police, is investigating the case and he is determined to catch the killer before the storm dies down.

The drama's highly stylised location is demonstrated in the opening title sequence – 12 intercut shots of decaying bodies, Icelandic landscape and rock formations, which are used to signpost to the audience the drama's crime-fiction motif. In an interview with artofthetitle.com, the director, Börkur Sigþórsson, explains that the opening title sequence to *Trapped* is an intimate minute of texture and tension used to symbolise a slow-paced culture and to set up audience viewing expectations for the drama.

The visual images in the sequence are accompanied by a musical theme played predominantly by stringed instruments creating an eerie orchestration of a bleak landscape and setting for the drama. The *Trapped* title sequence works to the conventions of long-form drama, in that it establishes expectations of what is to come.

The opening title sequence captures the essence of *Trapped* – a crime story where bodies keep turning up and crimes disrupt a peaceful Icelandic community – through the alternative themes of abandonment and isolation, reflecting a **verisimilitude** of a contemporary Icelandic community.

Trapped is unsettling in the most disarming way – a quiet and isolated costal town is the location for a brutal murder that the chief of police Andri Ólafsson describes as a 'disgusting' crime. The setting becomes a major player in the drama, a character in itself, mercilessly exerting itself upon those caught in its grip. The sense of hostility and entrapment in this hostile arctic environment creates another layer of suspense in the Nordic Noir storyline. This motif is crucial to the success of *Trapped*, enabling the programme makers not only to capture the essence of Icelandic culture, but also to package and sell it to **transnational** audiences.

Masculine representations

The narrative arc of *Trapped* pivots around the main character, a rugged Icelandic man who is presented as being at one with the harsh cold landscape. Episode 1 introduces this central character, burly police officer Andri Ólafsson, with small icicles clinging to his unkempt beard. He is chief of police in a town where everyone knows each other, and Ólafsson's initial scene places him in a domestic setting with his children and their grandparents (his parents-in-law). It is significant that he is introduced as a father and single parent first and then as the chief of police. His masculinity is defined by the roles he has as a father, protector and law enforcer.

Knowledge check 35

Which studio produced *Trapped*?

···

Knowledge check 36

What were the series production costs for *Trapped*?

···

Verisimilitude The appearance of being true or real.

Transnational Extending or operating across national boundaries.

The story centres on Ólafsson being a lone parent, restoring his house, identifying dead bodies and leading a police investigation into a serious crime. At first sight, as a bearded and overweight middle-aged man, he does not seem a typical representation of a police officer with heavy professional commitments, but in fact he is highly effective at his job. He is calm, at times emotionless, and shows anger only over his ex-wife, who has left the family to be with another man. Episode 1 reveals more about the complexity of his character, his functions as the chief of police, and his responsibilities and skills as a detective. For example, he quickly deduces that the body found by the fisherman has not been in the water for long and on inspection of the body he reveals the likely cause of death.

Ólafsson is also, in contrast, a devoted father to his children and treats others with respect. He communicates well, for example when dealing with the Danish captain who is obstructive about the initial investigations on the ferry, refusing to allow a search of the vessel without a Danish court order. That said, despite Ólafsson's affection for the surrounding landscape and being the only character constantly on the move and prepared for the arctic conditions, he is metaphorically trapped in this small coastal town that he loves. He is also trapped by the love he has for his ex-wife – he is still wearing his wedding ring – and finally he has his hands tied by the detectives and forensic team in Reykjavik. He cannot officially start his investigation into the murder until they arrive, but they are held up by the weather conditions. It now falls on Andri and his two less-experienced police officers to solve the murder case, which has a list of suspects that even includes the Eastern European human-trafficking mafia.

Audience theory and engagement

A central element in long-form TV drama is the way that it deals with complex characters, so opening up multiple audience readings of the text. Andri Ólafsson's entrapment can be read by the audience as a crisis in his masculinity. This can be contrasted with the dominance of male characters, which reinforces the traditional Icelandic representation of masculinity – the captain of the ferry is male, the mayor and town planners are male (and pivotal to what is to come in the town development subplot) and hold powerful positions in the community. In contrast the female characters, such as Andri's wife the school teacher (albeit she is no longer part of the family unit), still fulfil traditional roles in an Icelandic culture. Nonetheless Ólafsson is still able to manage an impending crisis in his beloved community as well as his role as chief of police while having to deal with emotional issues in his own family life.

Long-form TV dramas tend to offer diverse and contradictory representations that audiences can use to reflect on their own identities. This form of drama has both the screen time and resources to develop such complex representations. Gauntlett's theory (2008) on representation and identity suggests that the media have an important but complicated relationship with identities. In the modern world it is now an expectation that individuals make choices about their identity and lifestyle, and this is evident in the representation of masculinity in *Trapped*. Even in the traditional media, there are many diverse and contradictory media messages that individuals can use to think through their identities and ways of presenting themselves. In Andri Ólafsson this is expressed through his professional life as chief of police and his role as a modern

> **Study tip**
>
> If you are studying this episode in preparation for a written assignment, do use the content and specific examples as evidence to support your arguments and to help explain the points you want to make.

father, emphasising the positive and entrenched associations of 'Icelandicness' with maleness. The episode reflects a mostly traditional society where patriarchy is only partially contested: the community is governed by men – the mayor, the MP, the local businessmen, the police chief and the Reykjavik detectives are all men – suggesting a persistence of traditional gender roles, although the female police officer is represented as professional and she has agency within the narrative.

Ideology and national identity

The development of the storyline in *Trapped* is similar to the way in which narrative devices are used in other European long-form TV drama. The narrative arc of Andri Ólafsson as the police chief interwoven with his domestic life compares to Birgitte Nyborg in *Borgen*, for example. The story unfolds with the arrival of a ferry carrying tourists from Denmark and the body being found in the water by fishermen. Episode 1 is structured around the ferry using the port to offload tourists on their final journey to the capital city, bringing a sense of realism to events. It is also significant that the disruption to this Icelandic community comes from 'outside' – from the 'Bloody Danes' as they are referred to in the dialogue – offering a social political context of the rivalry in Nordic politics. The interweaving of Ólafsson's personal life and that of the community adds layers and texture to the equilibrium and exemplifies how melodrama sometimes sits alongside suspense in Nordic dramas.

The discovery of the body is the force that propels the investigation and signifies to the audience that this is a crime story. The audience are also introduced to Icelandic community and society and further potential disruptions: a subplot in which the mayor and politicians are looking for Chinese investment to redevelop the port of Seyðisfjörður and its community. Further disruption comes in the form of the weather, as the school is closed, and in the arrival of Ólafsson's ex-wife and her partner, for whom Andri appears to have very little time – he is preoccupied with the murder investigation of the dismembered body.

Episode 1 fits a lot into 50 minutes because it is setting up audience expectations both of how the story might develop and of the trials and tribulations that lie before Ólafsson. Other narrative devices include the use of a narrative flash-forward narrative (captioned 'seven years later'), where the male used in the opening scene is spotted on the ferry by Ólafsson. *Trapped* also uses typical conventions of the long-form TV drama, for example a narrative cliffhanger where the potential suspect escapes from the motorhome. This poses the questions, 'Where is this people-smuggler? What will happen to him and the passengers (a woman and a young child) who escaped from the back of the vehicle? How will they survive?' Such narrative hooks encourage the viewer to watch the next and subsequent episodes. This lack of narrative resolution is typical of the form and the way in which Icelandic TV drama repackages a successful formula for a global TV audience and in the process adds value by creating identities of Icelandic crime thrillers and the country itself. Other significant representations are political: the mayor and the Reykjavik politicians are in a planning meeting at the town hall discussing the future of the port of Seyðisfjörður.

Trapped displays some unique Icelandic elements that set it apart from the other Nordic crime series. One such element is the formidable presence of nature, which literally

> **Study tip**
>
> As long as you support your views with evidence from your study you can challenge theories of representation. As a reader of media texts, you need to apply academic ideas and not just reinforce them!

dictates the narrative course. For example, by the end of Episode 1 the arctic conditions actively help the murder suspect disappear into the landscape. These elements are also used as a narrative device to plot the search for the killer in subsequent episodes.

Trapped has become extremely important in its representation of Iceland to the outside world, as well as working to present Iceland as a tourism destination with a rich history in industry and fishing and highlighting its rivalry with Denmark. The representation of place in *Trapped* is not simply exotic – it is a reality constructed through the dramatic form, the ideological and values systems of which are packaged and exported around the world. European long-form TV drama often attempts to reach and engage an international audience by offering a local representation that has international resonance, thus increasing diversity in the media of representations of place and cultures.

The success of *Trapped* as a Nordic Noir is reliant on the representation of 'Icelandicness', delivered through its multi-layered text that reflects the social and political context of a local fishing port. By stylising the crime drama and structuring the narrative of the drama around the central character, the audience is offered a text with which to engage and negotiate meaning.

Deutschland 83 Season 1, Episode 1, June 2015

Deutschland 83 is an eight-episode German spy thriller series. It is a co-production of AMC Networks, an American Entertainment company, and RTL Television, a German television network. AMC Networks is dedicated to producing quality programming and movie content. In co-operation with companies such as SundanceTV (also part of AMC Networks) and RTL Television, it delivers distinctive, compelling and culturally relevant content that engages audiences across multiple platforms. AMC Networks is American Entertainment's global division, creating engagement with audiences and generating value for its advertisers.

Deutschland 83 reflects the highly competitive nature of US cable and satellite television, in which channels such as Sundance Channel seek quality programming to maintain the brand (for example by moving into international co-operation to produce and premiere foreign-language programming), and the reliance of German commercial broadcasters on international co-productions for prestige drama.

AMC is emerging as an international creative hub to serve the local TV landscape, which is shifting to authored, high-budget series. According to the co-creator of *Deutschland 83*, Joerg Winger: 'We're coming from a culture that doesn't have any German series in primetime and where all the time slots were 90 minutes. We don't have the tradition of serialised drama, or the same kind of writing culture as the USA' (http://broadcastnow.co.uk, May 2017).

Knowledge check 37

Which American production company co-created *Deutschland 83*?

Economic contexts and distribution

The distribution of the TV drama was in co-operation with FremantleMedia International in the UK and through SundanceTV in North America. SundanceTV focuses on the broadcast of independent and world cinema including documentaries and is a feeder for the Sundance Film Festival, a prestigious and established conduit for independent film production. The series was premiered on the SundanceTV channel in the USA in June 2015, becoming the first German-language series to air on a US network. This is an example of how global TV shows can be packaged by media companies to domestic markets.

The broadcast was in the original German language with English subtitles. It aired in Germany and on Channel 4 in the UK on 4 January 2016. *Deutschland* 83 became the most popular foreign-language drama in the history of British television, with an audience of 2.5 million viewers as of January 2016. The global distribution rights of *Deutschland 83* were attained by Fremantle, a British international subsidiary of Bertelsmann RTL Group and Europe's largest TV production company.

The first season of *Deutschland* 83 did not achieve high viewing figures in Germany and had weak initial ratings. Episode 1, entitled 'Quantum leap' and written by Anna Winger, achieved 3.19 million viewers, while in the UK Channel 4 attracted 2.16 million viewers and in America it attracted about 500,000 viewers. It was considered a **sleeper hit**, securing a second season in 2016. Amazon has negotiated the rights for a third season. The drama was also distributed in Ireland and Australia. Online services such as Sky Deutschland, Netflix and Amazon have further driven up the demand for premium drama in Germany. Young Germans are watching series online from all over the world, and they also want to see something that is from their own culture.

Sleeper hit A media product that becomes successful gradually, often with little promotion.

The production team for *Deutschland* 83 did extensive research, with experts from both former East and West Germany, to provide historical information and background. It was vital for the producers to create a historical spy drama that was as realistic a representation of the time period as possible. For this reason, the drama was shot in and around the following locations in Berlin:

- a suburb in east Berlin that was used to portray period East Germany
- the Stasi Museum, which is the actual site of the original Stasi headquarters.

Such locations were used by SundanceTV as part of its digital marketing strategy, which reflected its recreation of both East and West Germany in the early 1980s. SundanceTV built an online campaign with a dedicated website (www.sundancetv.com/shows/deutschland-83) that gave fans an interactive insight into what Berlin looked like back then versus now. Use of place and historical comparisons on **interactive sliders** encouraged audience engagement, allowing them to toggle instantly between the past and the present to witness the transformation in locations.

Interactive slider Image-based material combined with text and logo, inserted at the start of a drama.

NEWS ›

Exclusive: An inside look at SundanceTV's digital strategy for Deutschland 83

By **Natan Edelsburg** · 06 July 2015 13:00pm

SundanceTV is continuing to launch originals that are catching critics attention. Their latest show is German series that's in the middle of its first season (each episode airs on Wednesdays at 11 ET). Deutschland 83 is a "coming-of-age story set against the real culture wars and political events of Germany in the 1980s" and "follows Martin Rauch (Jonas Nay) as the 24 year-old East Germany native is pulled from the world as he knows it and sent to the West as an undercover spy for the Stasi foreign service."

Figure 2.6 The interactive sliders of *Deutschland 83*

This proved a very good strategy for marketing *Deutschland 83*. When interviewed about the show's digital strategy, Drew Pisarra, vice-president of digital media and marketing for SundanceTV, explained why such a digital initiative had been chosen:

> **Germany has undergone such major changes in the last 30 years that the slider felt like a very interesting, accessible and visually powerful way to spotlight that evolution. We're really pleased with how many people are coming online to engage with the *Deutschland 83* content and catch up on past episodes.**
>
> (Source: www.thedrum.com, 6 July 2015)

This clever use of a website, timed for the release of Series 1, established a fan base. The digital promotion of the show was filled with stylistic propaganda-style art, episode summaries and quotes, and references to popular music culture of the 1980s, the historical context for the period historical drama. Pisarra explained that: '… having co-creator Anna Winger tweeting out sharp, insightful running commentary each week during the initial East Coast broadcast adds to that mix' (www.thedrum.com, ibid.).

The success of the *Deutschland 83* marketing campaign's use of online technology in triggering audience engagement is symptomatic of how media institutions raise awareness of a product. Understanding how the drama is shaped by the production team in terms of its visual style and then through its promotion is vital. A drama's

Knowledge check 38

Which terrestrial TV channel broadcast the series *Deutschland 83* in the UK?

visual style is driven by its aesthetic (its artwork and design) and by the values that the drama promotes. For *Deutschland 83* this is its interpretation of historical events in East Germany in the 1980s, set against the real culture wars and political events in Germany at that time.

Historical and cultural contexts

Deutschland 83 is set in the 1980s, during the Cold War. This historical context provides the setting for the spy thriller, with the geopolitically and ideologically divided East and West Germany. Episode 1 introduces the audience to the strong East German Stasi official Lenora Rauch as she watches US President Reagan on TV at her government's embassy in Bonn, West Germany. Reagan denounces Soviet Russia as an 'evil empire'. The use of Reagan's real recorded political speech footage intertextually references the reality of the 1980s and the Cold War between two superpowers, bringing verisimilitude to the drama. This would appeal to older audiences who lived through this historical period, as well as providing the political and historical context for younger viewers of *Deutschland 83*.

Episode 1 continues with the introduction of Martin Rauch, an East German border guard, as he reprimands a pair of young students who have bought textbooks on the black market. He toys with them, saying they should be reading Marx rather than this Shakespeare, which he confiscates. His seriousness turns into laughter once the students leave and he jokes with his colleagues. Ironically, he presents the copy of the Shakespeare to his mother (Lenora's sister) upon returning home, hinting at corruption or possibly the scarcity of literature available in East Germany when it was part of the Soviet Bloc. East Germany remained part of the Soviet Bloc until the Berlin Wall was pulled down in 1989 and German reunification began.

The theme of scarcity in East German culture is reinforced throughout the drama, for example when a jar of coffee is given as a gift or when comparing the family homes of the two main characters, which are represented as binary opposites in the narrative. In terms of the settings, East Germany is considerably poorer under the Soviets than its affluent counterpart West Germany. Such binary opposites are useful when analysing representations and their ideological effect and for interpreting which side of a dichotomy is valued by the narrative. This is no more evident than when Martin Rauch first enters West Germany and he runs into the supermarket. The hyperbolic 'Wes Anderson-style' interior shots in the supermarket are overwhelming – Martin looks around in disbelief at the abundance and choice of neatly stacked groceries.

Media form and style

The narrative arc of *Deutschland 83* centres around Martin Rauch, who is 'recruited' by his aunt Lenora Rauch and her colleague Walter Schweppenstette. They are top members of the Stasi, the East German secret police. Martin Rauch is then trained in West Germany as a spy in basic espionage skills, teaching him how to pick locks, take hidden camera photos and secretly hand over documents. He is assigned to steal secrets from US army General Jackson and so becomes a ranking officer serving General Edel, under the false identity of Stamm. While General Edel and US General Jackson meet and then break for lunch, Stamm breaks into Edel's locked office and uses his microfilm camera to snap images of secret NATO documents. These are then passed on to another secret agent at a barbeque thrown at General Edel's house later that day.

Knowledge check 39

Who wrote *Deutschland 83*?

Knowledge check 40

Identify a location used for the shoot of *Deutschland 83*.

The classic espionage plot takes a twist when Martin Rauch is caught by General Edel's sister-in-law Renate Werner trying to contact his girlfriend at home in East Germany. Renate Werner is drugged so that Martin can escape detection. Believing he has completed his assignment, he meets Lenora to discuss returning home – but she has other plans, using his mother's illness and material bribery to persuade him to continue to act as a spy against West Germany and the USA.

Deutschland 83 falls into a spy espionage genre and has a clear and realistic historical setting. What makes it successful, however, is the way in which it uses the binary opposition in Cold War politics but is light-hearted in its approach. It is stylistically produced for its audience, focusing as much on entertaining the audience as on being a tense and suspenseful drama. Martin is represented as intelligent, resourceful and honest and is recruited much against his will, but these characteristics are blended with his role as a spy and deceiver. This juxtaposition of representations adds interesting depth to his character and the audience is positioned to sympathise, not with his actions as a spy serving East German interests, but with him being kidnapped and cajoled into spying. The audience identifies with his family life, which is interwoven with the espionage – his ailing mother awaiting a liver transplant, his girlfriend, his friendship group and the rich cultural way of life that he misses.

The audience is shocked that it is his aunt Lenora who causes this disruption to Martin's normal way of life or equilibrium. In *Deutschland 83* the narrative arc establishes a sense of normality for Rauch: the initial equilibrium is Martin's girlfriend, job and family life; the disruption is US President Reagan's escalation of Cold War conflict in Europe. Lenora 'blackmails' Martin into spying for his country by saying she will arrange for his mother to be put on a hospital list for a transplant. *Deutschland 83* combines politics, culture and family life to tell its story – which is enhanced by its reconstruction or reinterpretation of East/West Germany in the 1980s.

Figure 2.7 Martin Rauch in *Deutschland 83*

Remaking or recreating a time period involves invoking a realism, so that in this case the last few years of the Berlin Wall era come to life for both German and international TV audiences. This is achieved through:

- the drama's *mise-en-scene*
- its use of binary oppositions in the narrative – which may be hugely stereotyped but are effective in targeting sophisticated, 'media-savvy' audiences through highly localised representations of East–West relations and German spying
- its soundtrack, which relies on Euro pop from the 1980s to sell the drama to both German and global audiences.

The episode reflects the social contradictions in divided 1980s Germany: East Germany is represented as a rigidly controlled state that promotes women's equality, with Lenora as the powerful woman who sets up the spying operation; whereas in West Germany, which is less controlled, the military is represented as rigidly patriarchal. Both civilian Germanys are represented as white and the representation of the racial integration of the American military appears to add to its 'otherness'. The episode shows the influence of social anxieties about facing up to Germany's divided past.

Episode 1 of *Deutschland 83* explores the historical trauma of German division and looks towards reunification. The episode represents the division of Germany in 1983: the East is poor, controlled and firmly ideologically Soviet; the West is rich and free, but self-doubting. These complex and ambiguous representations reflect the difficulties that Germany continued to face in the 2000s when coming to terms with its divided past and, in particular, the political and military tensions of the early 1980s. It achieves this by examining the different ways of life being lived at that time, at geopolitical, societal and family levels. The values of these lifestyles are examined through the drama's characters and are engaged with by its audiences.

Summary

- Long-form TV drama is a concept that describes the recent shift of interest towards television series of high-quality drama.
- Comparing US and European long-form dramas reveals that some narrative devices are typical to both styles of drama.
- The study of long-form TV drama encourages examination of cultural texts from outside the UK and engagement with European media representations and issues.
- Long-form TV drama has become accessible to online audiences who are no longer constrained by traditional media output.
- The form has allowed its production teams the creativity to develop a unique cinematic style for these dramas.
- Narrative arcs are developed through long-form TV dramas, enabling complex characters to be introduced and allowing audiences to engage with them over time.
- Both US and European long-form TV dramas are polysemic texts that usually reflect a set of ideological values.
- Representations in long-form TV drama are reinforced, challenged and repackaged to the audience.
- Long-form TV dramas contain intertextual references and can be described as postmodern texts in that they offer the audience a galaxy of signifiers to decode.
- Long-form TV drama is distributed and consumed across digitally convergent platforms and so benefits from growing overseas audiences – on a global basis and with critical acclaim.

Practice questions and sample answers: Long-form Television Drama

3 Why do long-form television dramas represent social groups differently? In your answer you must:

- consider the context in which long-form television drama's representations can be understood
- explain how media contexts may have influenced representations in the set episodes of the two long-form television dramas you have studied
- make judgements and reach conclusions about the reasons for the differences in representation between the two episodes. [30 marks]

ⓔ In Question 3, the longer, comparative 30-mark question in Section B, you will be rewarded for drawing together knowledge and understanding from your full course of study, including different areas of theoretical framework and media contexts. You should have studied two long-form TV dramas: one from List A and one from List B (see Table 2.1 on page 46). Your answer should make reference to both of these long-form TV dramas.

In the sample essay below, the List A drama is *Homeland* and the List B drama is *The Killing*. Remember this is the longest response you will be required to write for the exam paper. Aim to spend 50–55 minutes on this question.

Sample answer

In addressing the question above I shall be comparing and discussing the US long-form television drama *Homeland* with the European long-form television drama *The Killing*. Through this comparison I hope to draw upon the different contexts in which long-form television dramas are produced and consumed by audiences and to offer explanation as to how such contexts may influence representations of gender and family in the set episodes. In reaching conclusions about the differences and similarities in these television episodes it is hoped that this essay will illustrate how the key media concept of representation can be used as an analytical tool in a global media environment to aid an understanding of the messages constructed within the conventions of long-form television drama.

Homeland was written as a response to 9/11 and the war on terror, and it interpreted their effect on the American psyche. *The Killing*, in contrast, was made to reflect how Danish life and representations are different to US-dominated conventional crime drama series. The programme makers of *The Killing*, while understanding the nature of TV crime drama, wanted to encourage a reading of victim and consequences not often told in formulaic crime dramas, and this can be related to the genre theory of Neale and the evolution of genre and how the programme makers wanted to develop a version of crime drama from a national Danish perspective drawing attention to processes of difference-within-repetition and hybridity in genre and long-form television drama. At the heart of both dramas is a female-centred narrative examining how these lead characters respond to crimes as investigators. Each story is told in relation to gender and race. *Homeland* is an American cable TV network show with a large budget, whereas *The Killing* was produced for state-run Danish TV and produced by one production company.

Both dramas share a sense of the melodramatic, albeit from different perspectives, and this is an example of how long-form TV drama experiments with the crime genre. In doing this, both use the theme of the family and family values so important to both US and Danish society. These readings of the text are offered to the audience in negotiation with the text: the melodramatic elements do not soften the issues but heighten the emotional realism of the victim (*The Killing*) or the reunited family (*Homeland*).

Despite the differences in their production budgets, US television dramas and European television dramas can influence representations due to more or less choice being available to programme makers when constructing representations, for example with regard to *mise-en-scene*, filming, sound and editing technology. *Homeland* with its large budget has a cast full of recognisable actors with whom audiences are familiar, whereas *The Killing* as a lower-budget national Danish drama used little-known actors and was shot in Copenhagen using the city and its locations as a source of its drama. Both dramas are highly stylised: *Homeland* offers fast-paced storytelling relying upon cinematic styles in its filming, while *The Killing* relies on lighting stylisation to replicate crime drama conventions and is slow-paced to develop emotional ties with the characters.

At the heart of both *Homeland* and *The Killing* is a discourse on the representations of gender in the main characters Carrie Mathison and Sarah Lund, as well as other characters. These roles are crucial to the crime/deception plots and, on occasion, both challenge and subvert gender representations to try and instigate cultural change and domestic conversations on representations and identity. Both female leads share certain generic traits in their representations across westernised television culture. As in Van Zoonen's argument about gender being performative, we see Brody's wife Jessica rehearsing being 'the good wife' while the army desperately tries to persuade Brody to perform as the masculine 'hero'. The CIA management figures are male, reinforcing patriarchal power, but the narrative follows the agency of a female protagonist playing the central role of a maverick whose intuitions are proved right. In *The Killing* the central female character Sarah Lund is represented as a career-minded single mother – a detective chief inspector who protects the innocent. Lund is calm, calculating and methodical in her police work. Her performance is admirable and she is the problem-solver and communicator.

In making judgements and reaching decisions about the reasons for the differences in representation between the two episodes, the conclusions are that although these are due in part to the contexts of production, with *Homeland* being a cable mainstream-produced US TV drama and *The Killing* being a Danish state-produced drama, the differences also require an understanding of how these contexts have affected the representations of gender and the family.

ⓔ The response makes a judgement and reaches a conclusion about the reasons for the differences in representation of family and society between the two episodes. The response attempts to address the key values and beliefs constructed by the TV dramas with consistent comparison. It is detailed and meets a high-level criterion. The response is convincing, offering perceptive and accurate analysis of representations in the set episodes for two long-form television dramas and consistently provides logical connections and a good line of reasoning.

4 **Evaluate the relevance of Todorov's theory of narratology to long-form television drama.**

[10 marks]

ⓔ Question 4, the shorter 10-mark question in Section B, requires you to evaluate the relevance of academic theories to long-form television drama. While Question 4 is the shortest on the paper, it is still demanding and requires a detailed response. Aim to spend 15–20 minutes on this question.

This practice question should apply Todorov's theory of narratology to the long-form TV dramas. You are expected to compare US and European dramas.

Sample answer

Narratology is a concept that allows for the study of a narrative's cause and effect; it deals with the structure and function of narrative, its themes and conventions. For example, in *The Killing* each day of the crime investigation is covered by one episode. Todorov's theory is useful for understanding different stages of how stories are told – while *The Killing* is a 'whodunnit' story, establishing a disruption to Danish society, *Homeland* is set up as crime espionage. Todorov's theory is helpful in teasing out the messages and values underlying a narrative – highlighting the significance of the transformation between the initial equilibrium and the new equilibrium. In *Homeland*, the following stages of Todorov's narratology are an equilibrium: the setting of the scene in Washington and the CIA, and establishing what life is like in a post-9/11 USA. We are also introduced to agent Carrie Mathison and her CIA colleagues.

The next stage to the episode storyline is the news that MIA marine officer Nick Brody has been found alive in the Middle East and will be repatriated. This is a celebratory story of a hero's return home. There is some disruption in these events throughout the story – his wife has a lover, his family is dysfunctional, and Carrie Mathison suspects he has been turned against his country – quite a controversial set-up for a story. In *The Killing* the disruption to the equilibrium is the murder – this is a force and different suspects are presented for the murder, for example Nanna's boyfriend, and links are found to the political party that owns the car her body is found in.

There is recognition of this disruption to the equilibrium, as Carrie Mathison, determined to investigate Brody's story, sets up surveillance in his house and looks for proof that he is messaging the terrorist cell. Mathison provides evidence to the CIA via televised coverage of Brody's heroic return that he is signalling to his terrorist cell through his body language – this complicates matters and the audience is left to consider what will happen next.

There is no resolution to the narrative because the nature of the long-form TV drama means that often storylines are worked out over a series of episodes, for example in *Breaking Bad* or *Mad Men*. European drama, like the Danish drama *The Killing*, often work with a lack of resolution or to a return to a new state of affairs in the last episode. This presentation of how the story is told is important to the media form and has helped to market and sell long-form TV drama to audiences globally and to promote binge viewing. Such narratives allow for deeper engagement with character and motive by the audience.

e The response demonstrates an adequate understanding of narratology and how both dramas establish characterisation and interweave and develop from the main linear narrative. It offers a generally accurate application of knowledge and understanding of media language to evaluate the usefulness of Todorov's narratology in analysing the media language of long-form television drama. It makes adequate use of textual examples rather than comprehensive coverage and so is a mid-level response.

Contexts grid for long-form television drama

Context	Long-form TV Drama
Historical	How long-form TV dramas are influenced by social, cultural, political and historical contexts through intertextual references. For example, *Stranger Things* and *Mr. Robot* are imbued with historical references of film culture. • Consider the historical context of production, for example *House of Cards* compared to *Borgen* as a political thriller reflecting contemporary political situations. • Societal influences including historically significant social events and contexts, for example *Homeland* and national security and *Borgen* and Danish politics. • Understand the reflection upon a historical period with the text, for example contemporary US fears of terrorism and national security in *Homeland*, or fears of immigration reflected in *Borgen's* storyline. • Ideological positioning – dominant and subjective political viewpoints and the tussle for power. • For US and European long-from TV drama, you should be able to locate the text according to place and culture, and the relevant locations in which the drama is set – for example *Trapped* is very much about Icelandic remoteness and culture. • Evaluate how the media products studied can act as a means of reflecting historical issues and events, for example *Deutschland 83* reflects a significant location and set of events.
Economic	How media products studied reflect their economic contexts through production, financial and technological opportunities and constraints. • Patterns of ownership. • Budgets and sources of funding – not available for all shows. Many US long-form TV dramas have very large budgets, compared to smaller European budgets. • Business models and free market competition – commercial success, such as viewing figures. • Public service funding and collaboration, for example in European long-form TV drama. • Subscription – new models of revenue not reliant on advertising, such as Netflix which produces shows like *House of Cards*. • Understanding public service remit, for example, *The Killing* or *Borgen*, and how these long-form TV dramas are funded as part of a national broadcasting strategy to sell a home product to a global market. • Independent and co-productions/collaboration of long-form TV dramas. • Size, scale and reach of production and distribution, for example the US long-form TV drama budget size compared to European forms. • Technology available and utilised including the influence of technological change, such as digitally convergent media platforms. • Above the line costs and below the line costs – marketing and distribution deals or the use of stars in long-form TV dramas.
Political	How media products can potentially be an agent in facilitating social, cultural and political developments through the use of media language to construct meaning through viewpoints, messages and values and representations of events and issues. • Contemporary societal events – *Borgen* and Danish politics could be contrasted to *Mr. Robot's* dystopian and undemocratic future. • Corporate versus the state – *Mr. Robot* again versus the state politics of *Borgen*. • Political perspective and bias, for example in *Homeland* in comparison to *Borgen*. • Ideals of national identity versus global perspective across all US and European long-form TV drama. • Ideology constructed in long-form TV drama including dominant, oppositional and hegemonic values. For example, US national identity and challenges to this, or the promotion of European identity and culture. • US versus European versions of democracy. • Constructions of verisimilitude in the long-form TV drama.

Social	How audiences consume and interpret long-form television dramas in different ways according to the narrative form. • Consider how long-form TV drama influences society and culture and the presence of societal discourse on, for example, politics, technology, gender and crime. • A consideration of demographic and technological factors related to consumption. • Consider how media language can be used to subvert or challenge genre conventions and a consideration of other factors such as genre hybridity, intertextuality, multiple narrative strands and fandom. • The media form – specific elements of media language used to create meaning such as camera shots, angles, lighting, settings, locations or cost. • The ways in which the narrative builds an audience in relation to the storytelling. • Reinforces social institutions such as the family, community, society and culture.
Cultural	How long-form TV drama affects audience consumption of cultural values. • Consider which cultural values are evident in the long-form TV drama and how these differ between US and European forms. • Whether any cultural capital is invested or challenged in the drama. • The social and cultural identities that are formed; for example, in relation to social groups including gender, ethnicity, age, national identity and religious beliefs. • Consider how social contexts reflect and may invoke discourse and ideologies and also how they may position audiences. • How audiences respond to and interpret media representations and how this reflects social and cultural circumstances.

Academic ideas for long-form television drama

Theory summaries

Industries

Curran and Seaton: Power and media industries

Studying television as an industry draws attention to issues such as:

■ the forms and effects of ownership and control

■ the working practices of creators

■ the issues of risk and profitability and critical appeal.

Applies particularly to the international dominance of the American streaming services distributing many long-form TV dramas. In prioritising the effects of ownership and control on the content of television, this theory may not help with understanding how ideologies, audience choice or media language conventions may determine media content of European long-form TV dramas.

Hesmondhalgh: Cultural industries

Draws attention to:

■ the forms and effects of ownership and control, such as the differences between the purely commercial American television products and the public service ethos of most of the European producers

■ the issues of risk and profitability in long-form TV dramas where high budgets are at stake and the ways producers will try to minimise these risks by using formatting – for example, genres and the star system

■ co-production deals for the smaller European broadcasters.

In prioritising the effects of ownership and control on the content of television, this theory may not aid in understanding how ideologies, audience choice or media language conventions may determine media content according to US and European based long-form TV drama.

Livingstone and Lunt: Regulation

■ Applies in part to long-form TV dramas produced by European public service broadcasters who may be regulated in the interests of citizens.

■ Applies in part to long-form TV dramas produced by American cable and streaming services that treat audiences as consumers and, at most, are only lightly regulated to avoid harm.

■ Draws attention to the challenge of globalised television industries to traditional regulation.

■ The study of OFCOM was from a national perspective, so only applies to the consumption of these long-form TV dramas in Britain or to British long-form TV dramas.

Audiences

Bandura: Media effects

■ May apply to a wide range of media products, including long-form TV drama.

■ Draws attention to the need to investigate the direct effects on individuals who consume long-form TV dramas.

■ Supports the arguments of those who think television should be regulated to avoid public harm.

- The complex and nuanced representations common to long-form TV dramas are less likely to cause a direct effect on audiences.
- Prioritising the effects of the media on the audience may mean that the effects of the audience on the media are underestimated.

Gerbner: Cultivation theory

- May apply to a wide range of media products, including long-form TV drama.
- Draws attention to the need to investigate the longer-term effects on individuals who consume long-form TV dramas, especially heavy 'box-set' users.
- Gerbner's investigations into the attitudinal effects of violent representations suggest that television programmes are possibly creating the belief in the audience that the world is a dangerous place, characterised by negative events.
- Supports the arguments of those who think television should be regulated to avoid public harm.
- The complex and nuanced representations common to long-form TV dramas are less likely to cause an indirect effect on audiences
- Prioritising the effects of the media on the audience may mean that the effects of the audience on the media are underestimated.

Hall: Reception theory

- May apply to a wide range of media products, including long-form TV drama.
- Draws attention to the range of different possible audience readings of a long-form TV drama's messages and values, while acknowledging the role of power in creating dominance within television messages and values.
- Does not explain anything specific to long-form TV dramas as it is a general theory of representation.

Jenkins: Fandom

- Applies particularly to the range and diversity of representations offered by long-form TV drama to 'textual poachers' who wish to use these products to create their own culture, for example via fan sites.
- Long-form TV dramas may achieve cult status, adding to their value for fans.
- This optimistic view of the power of audiences may underestimate the power of the oligarchy of media conglomerates to shape and control television content.

Shirky: End of audience

- Draws attention to the way audiences for long-form TV dramas can provide value for each other by using websites to offer comments, parodies, merchandise (for example, Sarah Lund sweaters) and so forth.
- Does not apply to broadcast television.
- Streaming services do not reflect the view of the online media proposed by Shirky insofar as they primarily operate like the 'old' media in offering centrally produced content.
- This optimistic view of the power of audiences may underestimate the power of the oligarchy of media conglomerates to shape and control television content.

Media Language

Barthes: Semiology

- Can be applied to any sign, including language and image, to tease out connotations and ideology.
- Useful for 'micro' analysis of media language.
- Does not explain anything specific to long-form TV drama as it is a general theory of signification.
- Less useful for analysing 'macro' media language elements such as narrative and genre.

- Does not tell us anything about the ownership and control of television and the process of mediation that leads to the messages in television.
- Does not tell us about how audiences interpret television and give meaning.

Todorov: Narratology

- Todorov's theory is sufficiently simple to be widely applicable, meaning that it is possible to identify the key elements – equilibrium (often implied) and disruption – in long-form television drama.
- Todorov's theory is very useful in teasing out the messages and values underlying a narrative, in pointing to the significance of the transformation between the initial equilibrium (displayed or implied) and the new equilibrium.
- It was not designed to explain long-form serial narratives but single narratives with resolutions, so does not explain complex narratives where climax and resolution are necessarily delayed and sometimes, in programmes that are designed to last many series, are never reached.
- Todorov's theory does not help to understand television's tendency towards segmentation rather than linearity, for example the multiple segmented storylines of some long-form TV dramas.
- Todorov's theory does not help to understand narrative strands that do not add to the narrative drive towards resolution but establish characterisation, nor does it help to understand narrative strands that spiral out from the main linear narrative or create cliffhangers.

Neale: Genre theory

- Was developed primarily to explain film genre, but can be applied to long-form TV drama as this is the most filmic form of television output, requiring an intertextual relay of pre-publicity and reviews to generate the large audiences required.
- Draws attention to processes of difference-within-repetition and hybridity in long-form TV drama.
- The theory of the shared code can be applied to the long-form television drama itself as a form – early versions of the form such as *Twin Peaks* established audience expectations of twisting and enigmatic narratives that have been developed through each addition to the generic corpus – despite the fact that these dramas range across various different genres.
- Many long-form TV dramas have the resources to rely on elements such as high production values, the star system, tone and exoticism rather than genre to market themselves, emphasising individual difference rather than generic similarity.

Levi-Strauss: Structuralism

- Can be applied to any cultural product, including long-form TV drama.
- Can be used to analyse long-form TV drama narratives by investigating, for example, how they set up an 'inside' and 'outside' opposition, asking the audience to identify with the inside, and then in some cases play around with this opposition to disorientate the audience.
- Can be used to analyse representations and their ideological effect, by seeing which side of an opposition is valued by the narrative.
- Does not explain anything specific to long-form TV drama as it is an extremely high-level theory of culture. Does not tell us anything about the ownership and control of television and the process of mediation that leads to the messages in long-form TV drama.
- Does not tell us about how audiences interpret television and give it meaning.

Baudrillard: Postmodernism

- Can be applied to any cultural product, including long-form TV drama.
- The theory may be celebrated in long-form TV dramas that refuse any simple identification of 'the real' in the fictional world (for example *Mr. Robot*).
- Does not explain anything specific to long-form TV dramas as it is an extremely high-level theory of the postmodern world.

Representation

Hall: Representation

- Can be applied to any media product, including long-form TV drama.
- Draws attention to the role of power in representations – both the general distribution of power in society and the power of the television industry – but also the power of the audience to decode representations in different ways.
- Does not explain anything specific to long-form TV drama as it is a general theory of representation.

Gauntlett: Identity

- Can be applied to any media product, including long-form TV drama.
- Long-form TV dramas may tend to offer diverse and contradictory representations that audiences can use to think through their identity as they have the time and resources to develop complex representations.
- Long-form TV dramas often attempt to reach and engage an international audience by offering a local representation with international resonance, thus increasing the diversity of representations of place and cultures, especially the successful non-English language long-form TV dramas.
- Long-form TV dramas may achieve cult status, adding to their value in helping create identities.
- Assumes that audiences are powerful, active agents, and so may underestimate the power of media conglomerates to shape popular culture, tastes, and identities.

Van Zoonen: Feminist theory

- Can be applied to any media product, including long-form TV drama, especially representations of gender.
- The concept of patriarchy may be applied to the ownership and control of television, the recruitment and ethos of television professionals, and the representation of gender in long-form TV dramas, especially the representation of women's bodies.
- Does not explain anything specific to long-form TV drama as it is a general theory of patriarchy.
- In prioritising gender inequalities, the theory may not aid analysis of other forms of inequality in representation in long-form TV drama.
- In stressing the influence of social conflict on representations the theory may underestimate the influence of social consensus on representations.

bell hooks: Feminist theory

- Can be applied to any media product, including long-form TV drama, especially representations of gender.
- The concept of 'intersectionality' draws attention to misrepresentations and stereotypes based on one or more of gender, race, class and sexuality, and their inter-relationship in any representations in long-form TV drama.
- Does not explain anything specific to long-form TV drama as it is a general theory of patriarchy.

- In prioritising gender linked to other inequalities, the theory may overlook similarities or equalities in representation in long-form TV drama.
- In stressing the influence of social conflict on representations the theory may underestimate the influence of social consensus on representations.

Butler: Gender performativity

- Can be applied to any media product, including long-form TV drama, especially representations of gender.
- Can be applied particularly to long-form TV dramas where the performance of gender is foregrounded, for example through representations of women preparing to present their bodies for display, representations of people training or reinforcing characters in masculinity, or representations that expose or disrupt heteronormativity.
- Does not explain anything specific to long-form TV drama as it is a very high-level theory of gender

Gilroy: Ethnicity and post-colonialism

- Can be applied to any media product, including long-form TV drama, especially representations of race, ethnicity and the post-colonial world.
- Gilroy draws attention to the continuing role of colonial ideology – of the superiority of white Western culture – across a range of representations in long-form TV dramas. Does not explain anything specific to long-form TV drama as it is a general theory
- In prioritising race and the post-colonial experience, the theory may not aid analysis of other forms of inequality in representation in long-form TV dramas.
- In stressing the influence of social conflict on representations the theory may underestimate the influence of social consensus on representations.

Glossary

ABC1 In media terms, an ABC1 audience is a demographic profile of an affluent media user, for example, defined by their social class—upper, middle and lower middle class. An educated audience.

Asynchronous viewing Viewing that does not happen at the same time.

Audience use and gratification An approach to understanding why, when and how people actively seek out specific media to satisfy specific needs.

BBFC (British Board of Film Classification) An independent organisation responsible for the national classification and censorship of films exhibited at cinemas and of video works, such as television programmes, released on physical media within the UK.

Beta version A version of a piece of software that is made available for testing, typically by a limited number of users outside the company that is developing it, before its general release.

Binge watch To watch multiple episodes of a television programme in rapid succession, typically by means of box set DVDs or digital streaming.

Branding The process involved in creating a unique name and image for a product or service.

Broadcast To transmit a programme or some information by radio, television or internet. Broadcast programming (scheduling) is the practice of organising and/or ordering broadcast media programmes in a daily, weekly, monthly, quarterly or season-long schedule.

Cel A thin clear sheet of plastic that a drawing is transferred to.

Cliffhanger A narrative device that creates a dramatic and exciting ending to an episode and leaves the audience in suspense and anxious not to miss the next episode.

Cloud computing Using a network of remote servers hosted on the internet to store, manage and process data, rather than using a local server or a personal computer.

Concentration of ownership A process whereby fewer individuals or organisations control increasing shares of the media.

Connote To suggest or imply meaning beyond a literal or principal meaning.

Console A specific device for playing video games.

Continuing serial A TV serial with a continuing plot that unfolds sequentially, episode by episode.

Cultural capital The social assets of a person (education, intellect, style of speech and dress, and so on).

Demographic A particular sector of a population.

Discourse A general term for a number of approaches to analysing written, vocal or sign language use, or any significant semiotic event.

Download The act or process of downloading data in the form of text, audio or video.

Film distributor A company that determines the marketing strategy for a film and the media by which a film is to be exhibited or made available for viewing; it may also set the release date and define the release windows – in cinemas, according to region, and then on digital services, DVD and Blu-ray, and ultimately on streaming services and free-to-air broadcasts.

Fourth wall A performance convention in which an invisible 'wall' exists between the actor and the audience. When an actor 'speaks' to camera, they are said to be 'breaking the fourth wall'.

Franchise A right to sell a company's products in a particular area using the company's name.

Gameplay The features of a video game.

Horizontal integration When a media company creates a chain of goods or services across different divisions, often subsidiaries of the same company.

Immersive experience Relating to time and energy or occupying one's attention.

Intellectual property rights The creation of rights to properties of the mind, including creative thoughts.

Interactive A two-way flow of information between computer users.

Interactive slider Image-based material combined with text and logo, inserted at the start of a drama.

Intertextual relay Genre codes and conventions established not just in media products but also in products that refer to or promote these products, such as critical writings, advertising and marketing material.

Intertextuality The interrelationship between texts – the way that similar or related texts influence, reflect or differ from each other.

Key fill lighting The use of lighting in a set-up where elements of the *mise-en-scene* have been filled with stark or contrasting lighting.

Licence fee A fee payable by the public for watching broadcast TV in the UK.

Licensing deal A legal contract between two parties, which grants a deal over a brand or product.

Media conglomerate A media group or media institution that owns numerous companies involved in mass-media enterprises, such as television, radio, publishing, motion pictures, theme parks or the internet. Conglomerates are usually global in their size and reach.

Media convergence The interconnection of information and communications technologies, computer networks and media content. It brings together the 'three Cs' – computing, communication and content – and is a direct consequence of the digitalisation of media content.

Media institution The underlying principles and values according to which many social and cultural practices are structured and co-ordinated by an organisation.

Media synergy Using a single-sourced idea to create multiple selling points and products.

Melodrama A sensational drama with exaggerated characters and exciting events; often overemotional.

Millennials A term widely used to refer to 18-35-year-olds.

Mini-major A film studio that, while smaller than the major studios, tries to compete directly with them.

Narrative arc An extended or continuing storyline in episodic storytelling media.

Narrative enigma A narrative code that entices the audience to watch the rest of the media text as they are curious about why things are not as they seem and what will happen next.

Non-diegetic Not a part of the real world of the text, for example added music that creates ambient sound.

Open-source software (OSS) Computer software with its source code made available; within its licence the copyright holder provides the rights to study, change and distribute the software to anyone and for any purpose.

Patriarchal Relating to or denoting a system of society or government controlled by men.

Playlist A list of recordings to be played on the air by a radio station; also a similar list used for organising a personal digital music collection.

Polysemic text The idea that any text can have multiple meanings rather than a single meaning.

Proliferation A rapid and widespread increase in use, in this case of technology.

Prosumer A consumer who becomes involved with designing or customising products for their own needs.

Public service remit The BBC is a public service organisation and serves the nation's interests. This public service remit is set out by Royal Charter and Agreement and at its core is the mission to inform, educate and entertain.

RAJAR (Radio Joint Audience Research) The official body that categorises and measures radio audiences in the UK.

Reboot Reimagining a previously made film as a fresh film, which re-invigorates the past film in order to attract new fans and stimulate revenue. Can be a comparatively safe project for a studio aiming for new audiences.

Sandbox game A game free of structure and constraint; players are free to roam and make choices about how they use the available content.

Shot-reverse shot A film technique where one character is shown looking at another character (often off-screen), and then the other character is shown looking back at the first character.

Signifier A sign's physical form (the term 'sign' in semiotics denotes an object, setting or event that indicates meaning).

Sleeper hit A media product that becomes successful gradually, often with little promotion.

Spin doctor A spokesperson employed to give a favourable interpretation of events to the media, especially on behalf of a political party.

Spreadability The wide distribution and circulation of information on a media platform.

Sting A sound or short musical phrase used on radio to punctuate the programme, for example to introduce a regular feature.

Subscriber A person who has arranged by payment to receive or access a product or service.

Subsidiaries Companies that are owned or controlled by another company, which is called the parent company.

Substitutability When a film shown in cinemas is then made available on DVD, as pay-per-view and on streaming/subscription services for audiences to consume.

Symbiosis A mutually beneficial relationship, or working hand in hand.

Synergy The extended impact of sequential media messages delivered by multiple media forms and/or where audiences are exposed to a sequence of advertising messages from a single source idea.

Textual poaching The appropriation by fans of media texts or the characters within them for the fans' own pleasure.

Time-shift In broadcasting, the recording of programming to a storage medium to be viewed or listened to after the live broadcasting, for example via BBC iPlayer.

Transnational Extending or operating across national boundaries.

Ultraviolet The industry standard digital code that enables the user to watch a programme on mobile and laptop devices.

User A person who uses a computer or network service.

Value chain How value is added to a media product in its distribution, for example in exhibition and by merchandising.

Verisimilitude The appearance of being true or real.

Vertical integration When a media company owns different businesses in the same chain of production and distribution.

Video game All games played on a console, phone or tablet as an app or on a computer, that incorporate the essential component of gameplay: interactivity.

Glossary

Video on demand Systems that allow users to select and watch/listen to programmes when they choose to, rather than having to watch at a specific broadcast time.

Voyeur A person with a general interest in spying on other people's private activities or moments.

Walk-and-talk scene Where the camera tracks the actions of the characters; often used for mini-plot summaries.

Web 2.0 A second generation of the world wide web, which is focused on enabling people to collaborate and share information online.

Windowing strategy A strategy used by producers and distributors to exploit their products. It involves segmenting global audiences by platform and territory, and rolling out television content across domestic and international markets through a series of sequential release windows.

Knowledge check answers

1 $100 billion vs $966 billion.
2 The production company is Walt Disney Studios and the cost to make it was $4 million.
3 Vertical integration is an arrangement in which the supply chain of a company is owned by that company, for example production and distribution. Horizontal integration is where a company develops by buying up competitors in the same section of the market.
4 Walt Disney Studios Motion Pictures.
5 A film distributor makes the film available to audiences, launches and markets the film, sets release dates, and provides digital copy in the form of DVD/Blu-ray and online streaming.
6 Any two of the points from the list from the *New York Times*: publicity stills (stars); film trailers (male/ *The Force Awakens*); product placement (Far East/ Hispanic audiences); use of social media (Facebook); Disney theme parks.
7 15–29-year-olds, and some programming for younger teenagers.
8 Nixtape; music artists, such as Sam Smith and Pink; video interviews and galleries available on *The BBC Radio 1 Breakfast Show* website.
9 To provide familiarity with the BBC as an organisation and to understand its scheduled programmes and remit.
10 6 million.
11 Four playlists: A gets approximately 30 plays per week; B gets approximately 15 plays; C gets approximately 6 plays; BBC Introducing gets 6 plays.
12 Any two from: Call or Delete; Nixtape; Happy Monday; Showquizzness; Happy Hardcore FM; Waking Up Song.
13 Any two from: iPlayer; Twitter; Facebook; YouTube (or Vevo); Instagram.
14 5.29 million listeners per week in 2017, compared to 5.7 million in 2016.
15 *Dwarf Fortress*, *Dungeon Keeper* and *Infiniminer*.
16 A game free of structure and constraint; players are free to roam and make choices about how they use available content.
17 To maximise profits and to improve the reach to new customers.
18 Mojang and $2.5 billion.
19 A digital distribution platform that offers digital rights management, multiplayer gaming, video streaming and social networking services.
20 Approximately 60 per cent.
21 Visual media content characterised by in-depth, lengthy narratives.
22 Amazon.
23 16.
24 13.
25 Predominantly male ABC1 subscribers.
26 2.8 million.
27 Crime thriller/espionage or political melodrama.
28 *E.T. the Extra-Terrestrial*. Through camera work, panning down from above.
29 When a media text makes reference to another text in a specific cultural reference or in reference to the conventions or style of a recognised genre.
30 Henry Jenkins.
31 For Denmark 1.7 million viewers, and for the UK 500,000.
32 Via the Danish website or the *Guardian* blog.
33 DR.
34 Judith Butler.
35 RVK Studios.
36 £7 million or 1 billion króna.
37 AMC Networks.
38 Channel 4.
39 Anna Winger.
40 East Berlin, or the Stasi headquarters (now the Stasi Museum), or West Germany.

Acknowledgements

The Publishers would like to thank the following for permission to reproduce copyright material.

Text credits

p. 7 OCR A Level Media Studies specification. Reproduced with permission; **p. 8, 12** OCR Media Studies Factsheet: The Jungle Book. Reproduced with permission; **p. 11** OCR Teacher Guide: The Jungle Book 1967 and 2016: Industries and audience. Reproduced with permission; **p. 15, 16** Extract from https://www.waxmarketing.com/imc-campaign-month-jungle-book/ © Wax Marketing, Inc. Reprinted with permission; **p. 21–22** taken from https://www.bbc.co.uk/aboutthebbc/insidethebbc/whoweare/publipurposes, used with permission from the BBC; **p. 30, 31** OCR Media Studies Factsheet: The BBC Radio 1 Breakfast Show. Reproduced with permission; **p. 37–40, 42, 43** OCR Media Studies Factsheet: Minecraft 2017. Reproduced with permission; **p. 40** Extract from This Is How Minecraft Irreversibly Changed Gaming—With Zero Funds for Marketing by Ryan Williams. Reprinted with permission; **p. 51** Reproduced with permission of Natalie Kane; **p. 54, 55** Excerpts from the Los Angeles Times article, "Binge-viewing is Transforming the Television Experience" by Dawn C. Chmielewski published February 1, 2013. Copyright © 2013. Los Angeles Times. Used with permission; **p. 56** Cynthia B. Meyers, "House of Cards Has No Advertising", Antenna: Responses to Media and Culture, Feb 14, 2013. Reprinted with permission; **p. 64** Stranger Things review – a spooky shot of 80s nostalgia straight to your heart by Lucy Mangan, Fri 15 Jul 2016 © Guardian News and Media Ltd. Reprinted with permission; **p. 67** Extract from To Spread or To Drill? by Jason Mittel, 25 February 2009, New York University Press; **p. 79** Interview with Joerg Winger, broadcastnow.co.uk, May 2017. Reproduced with permission; **p. 81** Interview with Drew Pisarra, http://www.thedrum.com/news/2015/07/06/exclusive-inside-look-sundancetvs-digital-strategy-deutschland-83, 6 July 2015, Natan Edelsburg. Reproduced with permission.

Photo credits

p. 8 © Everett Collection, Inc. / Alamy Stock Photo; **p. 11** © Disney/Kobal/REX/Shutterstock; **p. 15** © Rob Latour/BEI/REX/Shutterstock; **p. 23** © IR Stone / Shutterstock; **p. 34** © S McTeir/Hodder Education; **p. 35** © Magnus Hjalmarson Neideman / SvD / TT/TT News Agency/Press Association Images; **p. 58** © Netflix/Kobal/REX/Shutterstock; **p. 62** © Teakwood Lane Prods./Cherry Pie Prods./Keshet/Fox 21/Showtime/Kobal/REX/Shutterstock; **p. 66** © akg-images / Album / 21 Laps Ent / Monkey Massacre; **p. 69** © Moviestore/REX/Shutterstock; **p. 75** © RVK Studios; **p. 83** © RTL

Every effort has been made to trace all copyright holders, but if any have been inadvertently overlooked, the Publishers will be pleased to make the necessary arrangements at the first opportunity.